THE COURSE OF
HISTORY

A STUDY IN THE PEAK OF ELOQUENCE

AYATOLLAH MUHAMMAD MAHDI
CHAMSEDDINE

THE MAINSTAY FOUNDATION

Author: Ayatollah Sheikh Muhammad Mahdi Chamseddine

Translated and Edited by: The Mainstay Foundation

© 2015 The Mainstay Foundation

Printed in the United States.

ISBN: 978-1943393145

O my child, even though I have not reached the age which those before me have, yet I looked into their behavior and thought over events of their lives. I walked among their ruins until I was as one of them. In fact, by virtue of those of their affairs that have become known to me it is as though I have lived with them from the first to the last. I have therefore been able to discern the impure from the clean and the benefit from the harm...

From Imam Ali's (a) will addressed to his son Imam Hassan (a)

The Peak of Eloquence, Letter Number 31

CONTENTS

Contents

ABOUT THE AUTHOR

Ayatollah Sheikh Muhammad Mahdi Chamseddine was a prominent Shia-Lebanese religious scholar, intellectual, and public figure. He was one of the founders of the Supreme Shia Islamic Council in Lebanon, along with Sayyid Musa Al-Sadr and others. Chamseddine and Sadr were heavily involved in preaching a moderate understanding of Islam that espoused plurality and coexistence at a time when Lebanon was going through an extreme period of violent civil war. After the disappearance of Sadr in 1978, Chamseddine rose to the forefront as his successor.

Chamseddine was not only a religious figure, but a public intellectual and political thinker. He led Lebanon in its national and political introspection, always calling for inter-faith and intra-faith dialogue. He made the unity and advancement of Lebanon his priority through his calls for civic engagement, national sovereignty, and resistance to occupation. At the same time, his theory of political legitimacy was based on notions of social contract and popular sovereignty, as opposed to other prevalent Islamist ideologies at the time. I one of his most influential books *Nidham Al-Hukm Wa Al-Idara fi Al-Islam (The System of Government and Public Administration in Islam)*, Chamseddine set out his theory of national sovereignty based on Islamic teachings that gave religious legitimacy to representative government.

Chamseddine also played a central role in the establishment of the Islamic University of Lebanon, which became a leading institution in the country, including in fields such as surveying and biomedical engineering. The University is a member of the International Association of Universities and the Francophone University Association, as well as a number of other regional associations. Chamseddine also established a number of other institutions, including schools, orphanages, and social service organizations.

Chamseddine was born in Najaf, Iraq, in 1936 to a family known for religious and scholarly achievement. His father had migrated to Najaf to pursue his religious studies there. In 1948, while Chamseddine was still 12 years old, his father decided to return to Lebanon. Chamseddine stayed in Najaf to pursue his own religious education. During his stay of over 30 years in Iraq, Chamseddine studied with the most prominent Shia religious scholars, including Grand Ayatollah Muhsen Al-Hakim, Grand Ayatollah Abulqasim Al-Khoei, and Grand Ayatollah Muhammad Al-Rouhani. He rose to prominence in

Najaf and became a distinguished member of the seminary. In 1969, Chamseddine returned to Lebanon, where he began his illustrious legacy as a public figure. He survived an assassination attempt in 1990 and passed away due to illness at age 65 in 2001.

TRANSLATOR'S PREFACE

It was a great honor to have the opportunity to translate a book for a learned scholar and Muslim thinker such as Ayatollah Chamseddine. The book provided great insight into the movement of Imam Hussain (a) and its impact in changing history. May his soul rest in peace alongside the heroes who he dedicated his life to learn and write about.

Before our readers begin on the journey of this book, we hope that they keep a few important points in mind.

Firstly, there are great structural differences between the original Arabic language of the book and the modern English language. Such structural differences make the task of literal translation burdensome, and creates a final result that does not accurately capture the spirit and readability of the Arabic text. Because Ayatollah Chamseddine's work could not be encapsulated in a direct or literal translation, our translation method had to be oblique. Adaptations were used freely to capture the meaning of the text without being bogged down in the structural differences of the two languages.

The process of translation always begs us to find precise meanings for the passages that we translate. But when we encounter the majesty of the Holy Quran, we find ourselves incapable of understanding its intricacies, let alone translating its true and deep meanings. We turned to the works of translators who have attempted to do this before. Although no translation can do justice to the Holy Quran, we found that the translation of Ali Quli Qarai to be the most proper in understanding when compared to the interpretation of the text as derived by our grand scholars. As such, we decided to rely on Qarai's translations throughout this book, with minor adaptations that allowed us to weave the verses more properly with the rest of the work.

A second great limitation came with translating the narrations of the Grand Prophet Muhammad (s) and his Holy Household (a). Their words are ever so deep and ever so powerful. We attempted to convey these passages to the reader in a tone that is understandable without deviating from the essence of the words of these immaculate personalities. We pray that we were successful in this endeavor.

Finally, we want to take this opportunity to thank you for your support. As students of Islam and as translators of this text, our greatest purpose is to please God by passing along these teachings to others. By picking up this book, you have lent your crucial support to this endeavor. We hope that you will continue your support throughout the rest of this book, and we ask that you keep us in your prayers whenever you pick it up.

The Editorial and Translation Team,

The Mainstay Foundation

Author's Preface

History is the interaction of an object with its environment through time. In other words, history is the process of transformation, change and transition from one to state to another. Such a change occurs to an object or is achieved through its relationship with its surrounding elements over a period of time.

In the old prevailing view, this 'object' referred only to the human being. It referred more specifically to human activities: society and politics, military, social and cultural institutions.

History was the science of the human's interactions with his surroundings over time. The modern age, however, witnessed an evolution in the meaning of this term. Its meaning has been broadened to include everything in nature and in civilization: land, minerals, plants, animals, ideas, and science, among other human activities. It became possible for a historian with a comprehensive view of history to claim that history is like philosophy – a broad subject that encompasses all that is relevant to human consciousness.

Perhaps some of the great Muslim historians had to this same conclusion, giving history a comprehensive understanding that goes beyond human activities alone. These historians indeed included geographical or philosophical information in their historical writings. A good example appears in Al-Masoudi's book *Murouj Al-Thahab wa Ma'adin Al-Jawhar (The Meadows of Gold and the Metals of Jewel)*.

This comprehensive perspective, however, is not relevant to us here. Our attention is focused on the human history. Perhaps all other branches of history can relate to the human history through the lens of the modern comprehensive perspective, where some of man's activities (the history of science, arts and literature, philosophy) or his environment (plants, animals, earth layers) are chronicled.

History in this context is the human's action within his surrounding through time. It may address his actions in a particular community or within the boundaries of a particular culture. It may even expand to address human action on a global scale.

There is no doubt that the global perspective of the Muslim historians was acquired from the Holy Quran, which examines the capricious actions of nations and peoples. They also benefitted in strengthening their global outlook from the "genealogy" that they inherited from the old pre-Islamic custom, which then entered, like other Arabic and Islamic knowledge, the era of recording. Historical truth in genealogy is not the important part here, as it itself is prone to doubt. Rather the significance here is what the knowledge of kinship provides about the interdependence of people, tribes and internal relations. This realization extends the historian's insight to a wider scope beyond limits of geography, tribalism or national belonging.

* * *

With this wider scope, Imam Ali ibn Abi Talib (a) dealt with history, not as a historian but as a man with multiple dimensions. He was a man of doctrine, one with a divine mission. He was a statesman and he was a ruler. He did not reserve the use of history for preaching material; rather he utilized it in political discourse and criticism. He incorporated it in the cultural development and guidance of society. In addition, he embedded it in the continuous education he provided for the community.

In this book, we try to understand Imam Ali's (a) perspective on the impact of history and discover his methods for dealing with history through his public, intellectual and political life.

The main source of these studies is the Peak of Eloquence. We also used other texts not included by Sharif Al-Radi in this book to arrive at more details about the Imam's historical perspective or to complete some texts cited in a truncated manner in *The Peak of Eloquence*.

We hold *The Peak of Eloquence* as a document of great value in Islamic culture and civilization, from both the intellectual and political dimensions. Our only regret is that Sharif Al-Radi, may God rest his soul, had included texts for their aesthetic value favoring texts with artistic eloquence above all else. This may have also steered him to select parts of a text with those features while omitting the rest of the same text. The name that Sharif Al-Radi gave the book summarizes the purpose of his collected texts and infers the method he used in the collection process. Though a great work in itself, it nonetheless deprived Islamic civilization from an abundance of great knowledge and perspective that was not included merely for its less than poetic style.

Perhaps this was foreordained so that this information is subjected to close scrutiny to distinguish the authentic parts from the fabricated ones and so that this information can be organized by topic. Scientists and researchers would go to explore the books of biography, history, narration, literature, and all that was told on behalf of The Commander of the Faithful (a). Then the filtered parts can be combined with what is included in *The Peak of Eloquence* by Sharif Al-Radi. They could all then be classified and organized in a scientific manner within their respected topics. This would include politics, thought, preaching, war, jurisprudence, theology and other beliefs, among other topics. This would make The Peak of Eloquence and its addendum an excellent resource of great value and benefit for scientific studies.

The late Sheikh Hadi Kashef Al-Ghitaa' wrote a book *The Addendum to The Peak of Eloquence* and arranged it in the same manner that Sharif Al-Radi organized his book – speeches, books, and governance. However, this book falls short of our aspirations for two reasons. First, this book does not include everything that was neglected by Al-Radi or from which he deviated and therefore the need for a more comprehensive work remains. Second, it seems to us that Kashef Al-Ghitaa' included in his book all that was attributed to the Imam without subjecting the content to scrutiny. Thus, he included some texts that were attributed to the Imam which we believe were actually fabricated.

Confusion about the collected texts in *The Peak of Eloquence* is borne at times out of prejudice and other times out of ignorance. The confusion comes from two things: one, doubting whether the text is appropriately attributed to the Imam; or two, deeming the text inappropriate and casting it away as being falsely attributed to the Imam. It is relevant to point out that, in general, the confusion raised about the validity of crediting the collected texts to Imam Ali in The Peak of Eloquence has ended, or should end, with the general acceptance of these texts as belonging to the Imam. Since the documented research and studies conducted through *The*

Interpretation of The Peak of Eloquence (Shareh Nahj al-Balagha) by Izz al-Din ibn Abi al-Hadid (d. 656 AH), and up until present time, convincing answers to all of the raised questions have been provided. It put an end to all doubts on the propriety of attributing the content of The Peak of Eloquence to Imam Ali (a), to the extent that is sufficient to correct the historical crediting of any text in Islamic thinking.

The research and studies mentioned are divided into two groups:

1. Some follow the approach of internal scrutiny whereby the texts were examined for sentence structure and correlation between sentences, the types of vocabulary and metaphors used, and other such components of text. Ibn Abi Al-Hadid followed this approach in a number of instances of his interpretation of the book. Other researchers and interpreters used the same approach as well. This style of research is implemented infrequently and is limited to only some of the text from the book; therefore, there is an urgent need for a more comprehensive study of all of the text in The Peak of Eloquence with a similar approach.

2. Other studies used the approach of external scrutiny whereby sources, containing texts from The Peak of Eloquence, that came after Sharif Al-Radi were sought.

The result from both approaches was to generally confirm the appropriateness of crediting texts in The Peak of Eloquence to the Imam.

Perhaps the latest significant and comprehensive study based on external scrutiny belonged to Sayyid Abdul Zahra al-Khatib, published in his book *Masadir Nahj Al-Balagha wa Asaaneedah (Sources and Documentation of The Peak of Eloquence).*

This study will not be the last of its kind. Other studies will be added to what has been achieved in this field so long as there is growth in the publication of books on Islamic thought; these books which are still being written and distributed to libraries worldwide.

* * *

I would like point out that this study about the impact of history through the eyes of the Imam Ali (a) is part of a series of studies on The Peak of Eloquence, preceded by our book Studies in The Peak of Eloquence, which included four subject areas:

1. Society and Social Classes
2. The Rule and the Ruler
3. Matters of the Unseen
4. Preaching

A fifth subject area was added in the third edition titled: Enjoining the Right, Forbidding the Wrong and The Silent Majority.

* * *

I have benefited from the book *Al-Kashif 'An Alfath Nahj Al-Balagha fi Shurhoohah (Delving into The Interpretation of The Peak of Eloquence)* by Sayyid Jawad Al-Moustafawi Al-Khurasani. This is a book of great value and significant benefit to researchers. We hope that the author would improve on it by including more explanations in the new future editions and more texts from *The Addendum to The Peak of Eloquence*.

All praise is due to God, Lord of the Worlds.

Muhammad Mahdi Chamseddine

PART I

HISTORY AND GUIDANCE

HUMAN DEVELOPMENT

History is the impact of a being on time and space. A being is a plant, an animal, a human being or an inanimate object. The history of the plants, animals and inanimate objects evolves according to fixed laws outside of this realm. Inanimate objects did not create the rules for their movements; and thus, they did not create the rules for their own history. The same can be said of plants and animals.

The existence of all three of these creations is always subject to the principle of necessity. Therefore, all facets of their history are subject to the principle of necessity. Their history is the outcome of their necessary presence in time and space. As such, errors in the history of these creations are unconceivable because they are not in control of their actions and would thus be unable to determine their own history. Humans present a different scenario.

Human beings deal with the universe on the basis of the principle of choice. They are creatures with free will and not subject to the principle of necessity, with the exception of the biological processes in their physiology. Therefore, humans participate in creating the rules that impact their time and space. When they are unable to modify nature to their benefit, they are able to adapt in order to be in harmony with nature.

Humans love and hate, hope and despair, and suffer and dream. Humans also experience fear. They fear the unknown and they fear the future. Most importantly, humans think. They analyze the situations and the problems they face and synthesize them. They evaluate possibilities, weigh options, make choices and act based on those choices. As such, and through their actions, humans respond to their external and internal worlds from the standpoint of choice, and not necessity, given that they are creatures with free will.

Hence, with their free will comes error in analysis, synthesis and selection, and regression. Such effects lead to disappointment in their plans and projects, being an inherent part of the impact of humans on history.

Therefore, just as the history of humans is a bright and honorable record of victories and achievements in society and nature, it is also a miserable rap sheet full of their mistakes, setbacks and disappointments.

* * *

The gravest mistake man can make is to assume that he is often right and that his history is a straight line, always going forward, always progressive, fruitful, correct and free of errors or deviations. Another mistake man makes is to assume that his past is full of errors and failures, undeserving of attention or consideration, or that he has found the proper perspective in his present and that his direction towards the future will be constantly correct and successful. Both of these assumptions drive man to commit more mistakes and to face further misfortunes and disappointments.

When man thinks that his impact on history is always right, he eliminates all human contribution. He submits himself to the impact of human history as if it were subject to the principle of necessity like that of plants, animals and inanimate objects. He then commits major mistakes believing he is right. He furthers his mistakes with more oversights, which cause humanity added regression and cause greater individual and collective misfortune.

The same situation occurs when man judges his past as full of mistakes committed by his predecessors, caused by ignorance, misunderstanding and improper guidance. As such, he assumes there is nothing in this past that could be of use for the present or the future. He assumes that he was lost and he has found his way. Now he owns the truth that was lost to him due to his past that confined and paralyzed him.

By taking this position, man deems all of his past experiences as worthless failures. Without a doubt, this position is deliberately unfair. The truth is there is a lot of good in the experience of the past. Humanity has suffered various forms of pain and sacrifice. It has endured great hardship for the sake of discovering itself.

Either of these perspectives lead man to view himself and his present state, along with his current political and social institutions, with absolute unjustifiable confidence. Whether he unequivocally rejects his past or believes that history is infallible, such a man sees himself and his situation through eyes of hollow arrogance. Perhaps it is these two groups of people whom God speaks of here:

> *Say: Shall We inform you of the greatest losers in (their) deeds? (These are) they whose labor is lost in this world's life and they think that they are well versed in skill of the work of hands. These are they who disbelieve in the communications of their Lord and His meeting, so their deeds become null, and therefore We will not set up a balance for them on the day of resurrection. Thus it is that their recompense is hell, because they disbelieved and held My communications and My messengers in mockery.[1]*

---

[1] The Holy Quran, 18: 103-106.

This hollow arrogance and unqualified confidence lead man to commit grave mistakes. They threaten societies, and even humanity, with countless disasters never seen before in history.

This is what has happened to man in modern civilization and woe to him for what he created for his future.

* * *

These two extreme perspectives of history and the future have created an incomplete understanding of human progress. As a consequence, man was pushed to commit further blunders towards himself and his world.

In modern civilization, progress is measured only on a materialistic scale. In any society and under any political regime, progress is measured by production and consumption volumes in relation to the tangible things in life: food, clothing, housing, accessories, means of transportation, energy, roads, and entertainment. This is in addition to items used for facilitating the daily life at home and work, factories, weapons, and governmental and civil institutions that regulate all these operations.

This concept of human progress does not necessarily give any value or weight to the ethical wellbeing of man. Nor does it necessarily prioritize ethical values, which should guide his behavior in all facets of one's social, family, and work life.

The material concept is the guide for the ideas, plans and operations of national and international institutions related to development. Specialized agencies in the United Nations, universities, international and national centers of research all measure the levels of progress and growth with this criterion.

As a consequence, amazing progress was achieved in the field of tangibles; progress that exceeded the wildest dreams at the beginning of the modern industrial revolution. But this progress was accompanied with a tragic regression in spirituality. Some forward-looking insights in the Western world, and perhaps the Eastern world as well, have started to uncover this issue and its seriousness, and they are warning of its disastrous consequences. In light of this understanding of progress, in the 1950s, the human race was divided into three worlds:

The first world: North America, Western Europe, and Japan. They have reached the highest level known by man in organization and materialistic progress.

The second world: The Soviet Union, Eastern Europe, and "finally" China. According to the above definition, these follow the first world in rank and they are working hard to catch up with it in the various fields.

The third world: Asia, Africa, and Latin America. This part of the human race is called the underdeveloped or the developing world.

The third world carries the stigma of underdevelopment according to this concept and according to the progress standards based on this concept; these standards that are imposed by the modern civilization's thinking and influence. The people of Asia, Africa and Latin America rushed towards this perspective of human progress to catch up with the first world; a world which prevented them from achieving that goal by building on their own superiority, exploiting the third world's weaknesses, looting their wealth, and creating a chaos in their political life. In an effort to get rid of this persistent image of underdevelopment, the third world countries keep moving forward thinking that they are on the path of progress, while sacrificing many of their values and ethics and abandoning their principles, aspiring to have their people become a copy of those in the first world.

* * *

But this concept of human progress is inadequate because it only represents one aspect of the human condition. Taking this approach alone on human progress is one of the biggest intellectual errors made by man in modern civilization. It was taken because of man's erroneous outlook on history and the future, for the progress of a human being is essentially tied to his moral and ethical condition. This truth has finally been realized in modern civilization. This realization brings hope even though so far it has a narrow scope.

Some voices started to rise, here and there, within modern civilization. Scientists, poets, and intellectuals with deep insights from the elite of the Arab world, have forewarned of this erroneous outlook and its deadly consequences. They call for the adoption of another perspective that promotes balance between materialist aspirations and moral and spiritual progress. This elite group cautions that the continuation of civilization in exclusive materialism will lead to its dilapidation and the destruction of humanity, or at least a large part of it.

These bright minds with futuristic outlooks in the Arab world, and perhaps the Eastern world entirely, are close to the Islamic outlook in regards to the issue of progress and regression. However, we emphasize the existence of great differences related to the details of this outlook and to the adopted means and methods.

Islam, represented by the Holy Quran, the Prophetic Tradition, and jurisprudence, pushes man towards a better future starting from his present and past. It stresses a better future should be based on a combined approach giving an essential role to each, both material and meaning, towards achieving an integrated healthy life. The human impact on time and space must strive for progress and be complementary to material, moral status and human qualities so its impact is indeed progressive.

God Almighty says:

And seek by means of what God has given you the future abode, and do not neglect your portion of this world, and do good (to others) as God has done good to you, and do not seek to make mischief in the land, surely God does not love the mischief-makers.[2]

And He also says:

O children of Adam! attend to your embellishments at every time of prayer, and eat and drink and be not extravagant; surely He does not love the extravagant. Say: Who has prohibited the embellishment of God which He has brought forth for His servants and the good provisions? Say: These are for the believers in the life of this world, purely (theirs) on the resurrection day; thus do We make the communications clear for a people who know. Say: My Lord has only prohibited indecencies, those of them that are apparent as well as those that are concealed, and sin and rebellion without justice, and that you associate with God that for which He has not sent down any authority, and that you say against God what you do not know.[3]

The achievement of materialistic progress alone while neglecting the moral and ethical status of humanity does not suffice. Nor does restricting attention to the moral and spiritual

---

[2] The Holy Quran, 28: 77.
[3] The Holy Quran, 7: 31-33.

status while neglecting the affairs of materialistic progress serve all encompassing benefit. Neither of these positions represents a balanced perspective upon which the human impact on history must be based and the institutions of civilization built. Either of these directions alone represents a deviation, which does not serve humanity well nor does it build civilization.

In accordance with a balanced perspective, backwardness can come from both a lack of material progress and a disregard to moral and spiritual wellbeing. The following are manifestations of such regression: increase in crime across society, family disintegration, neglect to proper personal relationships, a substantial increase in warmongering and aggression within societies and between national groups, indifference to human life especially when the individual is considered outside the national or racial circles of the aggressor. There are numerous other manifestations of the corruption of the moral status of human beings at the individual, group, societal and country levels.

Moreover, according to this balanced perspective, it is a mistake to divide today's world into an advanced class of nations and an underdeveloped one. According to this perspective, all of today's world is underdeveloped. If the third world is falling behind with regards to the level of substance and methods of organization and management, the other world is falling behind in terms of its ethical status, human relations and the human values of its members, groups and communities.

Through this study, we will see the logical reasoning of the Commander of the Faithful Ali ibn Abi Talib (a) and his deep understanding of history. This is coupled with his firm grasp of the past and present human impact on the future, harmoniously based on this balanced outlook that Islam embraces. The Holy Quran and the prophetic traditions express this outlook; and thus, the jurisprudence follows suit as it is the derivative product of the two.

IMAM ALI IN THE FACE OF HISTORY

The Commander of the Faithful Ali bin Abi Talib (a), as we will see throughout this study, focuses heavily on history. This focus manifests itself in the expression of his ideas and thoughts on a wide array of topics.

The Imam's interest in history is not that of a storyteller searching for a captivating novel, nor is it that of a politician probing for tricks and tactics of pretext with which he can pacify a grumbling public. On the contrary, his interest comes as a progressive leader and futuristic thinker with a message, mission, and doctrine.

A storyteller looks for material of entertainment and excitement in the history of people. A politician searches history for methods to use in his daily political work to face dilemmas or to assist him in the development of immediate short-sighted plans.[1]

A historian offers both groups the historical material that meets their needs. The enlightened pioneer, the visionary, the true statesman, looks in history to find the roots of the human problem. He explores the past and present human efforts in this regard to resolve this problem. He strives to enhance humanity's capacity to reach its full potential – both spiritual and materialistic. This is coupled with a desire to enrich the human ability to achieve happiness while preserving human purity.

Imam Ali dealt with history in this spirit and through this perspective. He would only stop at the details of events insofar as they held evidence and symbols. Rather the Imam dealt with historical issues with a general holistic overview. Hence it is rare to observe the Imam discussing partial facts or events in his speeches or books. Instead his approach to history is characteristic of high-level overviews and inclusion.

---

[1] Al-Masoudi said in his report about the daily activities of Muawiya bin Abi Sufian, "… and he spends a third of the night on the news of the Arabs and their days, the foreigners and their kings and policies towards their people, the biographies of kings of nations and their wars and schemes, and their policies towards their people among other news of past nations…. Then he brings notebooks containing biographies of kings, their news, wars and schemes and has young men, whose task is to read and memorize these notebooks, read them to him. And so every night, he would hear some of the news, stories, impact and types of policies…" Mourouj al-Dhahab (as researched by Mohamad Muhyiddin Abdul Hamid), al-Sa'ada Printing, second edition (1367 AH – 1948 AD), third volume, p. 40-41.

The Imam is not a historian and thus it is not expected for him to adopt a historian's perspective or style in recounting and analyzing facts or judging their content. Rather he was a statesman, a leader, and a life-long visionary. He dealt with history as an element that shapes the character of the present and the future. Therefore this impact occupied a significant role and a highly critical level of risk in the both education and political life. This is what makes a man with a message and a leader such as Imam Ali (a) try to enter into the consciousness of his nation. He held himself responsible for leading his nation and its fate. Thus, providing a proper view of history was a priority for him and would be a constructive strength, not a destructive or corruptive one.

* * *

Imam Ali's (a) great attention to history was shown in the text of his will written in "Hadreen".[2] He wrote the letter upon his departure to Saffeen and addressed it to his son Imam Hassan (a). In it he said:

---

[2] Ibn al-Hadid said in his "Explanation of Najuh al-Balagh": 16/52 – "In regards the him saying 'he wrote it to him in Hadreen,' in the old days, 'Hadreen' had a different meaning and it meant the dual regions of present day Aleppo and Kansareen and this includes the meadows and the surrounding suburbs. We later presented this term to a group of sheikhs who could not offer an explanation. Some of them assumed it was a plural, not dual form. I searched for this word in many books from all over the world and I could not find it. Perhaps I will find it later and I will append it to this work when I do."

Sheikh Mohamad Abdoh said in his explanation: "Hadreen: The name of a town in the region of Saffeen."

My son, though I have not lived as long as those before me, I have studied their work, reflected on their stories, and walked in their footsteps, until I became one of them. It seems as though because of my exposure to so much of their affairs as if I have lived with them from their first until their last. I have come to distinguish the purity of this perspective from its turbidity, and its benefit from its harm.

In the same will he directed Imam Hassan (a) to study history for the moral lessons and advice therein. He said:

Revive your heart with advice... and show it the stories of the old people and remind it of their fate. Walk in their hometowns and see the evidence of their existence. See what they have done, where they ended up, where they had arrived and where they had settled. You will find that they left their loved ones behind and they lived in foreign lands. By doing so, it would be as if you have become one of them.

This text leads us to believe that the Imam (a) frequently talked about historical matters in his political guidance and intellectual upbringing of his community, and to the men in his administration and his companions. However, the political and intellectual texts that included historical elements mentioned in the Peak of Eloquence were very few. This is with the fact that the sermons that were built on historical observations were relatively many.

We cannot fully explain the lack of the political and intellectual historical texts except by assuming that these texts could have been lost because they were forgotten by the narrators, or they were omitted by Sharif Al-Radi in his compiling of the Peak of Eloquence. His approach in writing his book was to "select the best of speeches, then the best of books, and then the best of quotes and literature."[3] This approach naturally led to the omission of many of the political and philosophical texts because these were not written with the utmost of eloquence and pithiness.

It is also certain that a lot of the Imam's words on this topic and others did not reach Sharif Al-Radi as he himself admitted when he said:

> ... *In spite of this, I do not claim that I know all that the Imam (a) said and that none of his words had escaped me. I do not doubt that I have missed more than I have gathered and whatever I missed is beyond my abilities.*[4]

* * *

In any case, the important question that we encounter here is: Where did the Imam derive his historical knowledge?

---

[3] From the introduction of The Peak of Eloquence by al-Sharif al-Radi.
[4] From the introduction of The Peak of Eloquence by al-Sharif al-Radi.

He says about himself: "I have studied their work, reflected on their stories, and walked in their footsteps..." What were the means he used to get to know their work so he could consider it and how did he get insight into their stories so he could contemplate them?

We believe that the Imam (a) acquired his historical knowledge from different sources:

THE HOLY QURAN

The Holy Quran is at the forefront of sources from which the Imam drew his historical knowledge. The Quran includes many historical texts scattered among the contents of the chapters with stories of ancient nations, their rise and fall and the extinction of many of them. This came through the Holy Quran's accounts of the prophets throughout the history of mankind. This is in addition to the narration of how every nation and people responded to the God's messages heralded by the prophets (peace be upon them all).

The Commander of the Faithful Ali (a) was the most knowledgeable, after the Prophet Muhammad (s), of the Quran's contents. This includes the apparent and the hidden, the clear and the ambiguous, the abrogating and the abrogated, the goals and the objectives, the present and the future implications, among other matters from the Quran. His knowledge of the Quran was comprehensive, encompassing everything closely or loosely related. In addition, the Quranic influence is very clear in the historical thinking of the Imam in terms of the approach and the content, as it is also very clear in all other aspects of his thinking.

The Imam described himself with regards to this feature of his personality, revealing that he would persistently inquire with the Messenger of God (s) about the Quran and all of its dimensions. He said: "By God, no verse was revealed and I did not learn why and where it was revealed. My Lord bestowed upon me a reasoning heart and an inquisitive tongue."[5]

Many of his contemporaries testified in this regard. Some are narrated by Abdullah ibn Masood, he said: "The Quran was revealed in the seven letters, each of these letters has an apparent and a hidden meaning, and Ali bin Abi Talib (a) has knowledge of both meanings."[6]

PRIVATE EDUCATION

The private education with which the Messenger of God (s) favored Ali is another source for his knowledge, historical and otherwise.

---

[5] Ibn Saad: "Al-Tabakat al-Koubra" volume 2, part 2, p. 101. Al-Mouttaqi al-Hindi: "Kanez al-Oumal" 6/396. He said: "As said by Ibn Saad and Ibn Asakir, they said 'an eloquent and inquisitive tongue' and Abu Naim: Helyat al-Awleeya' 1/67.

[6] Abu Naim: Helyat al-Awleeya' 1/65.

Stories by narrators, biographers and Muslim historians of different sects and preferences all agree that the Messenger of God (a) singled out the Commander of the Faithful Ali (a) with a level of tutelage that he did not see worthy for any other member of his household or his companions.

This is what led Abdullah ibn Abbas to say: "By God Ali ibn Abi Talib (a) was given nine tenths of the knowledge and by God he has shared with you the remaining tenth."[7]

It is narrated that the Messenger of God (a) said: "Ali is the vessel of my knowledge."[8]

Anes ibn Malik narrated: "It was said, 'Messenger of God, tell us about whom should we write the knowledge?' He said: 'About Ali and Salman.'"[9]

Imam Ali (a) said: "The Messenger of God (a) taught me a thousand gates of knowledge; every gate leads to a thousand others."[10]

He expressed this on several occasions seen in the texts included in the Peak of Eloquence, where he said:

1. "… I have hidden knowledge, if I disclose it you will start trembling like ropes in deep wells."[11]

---

[7] Assal al-Ghaba 4/22 and al-Estee'ab 2/462.

[8] Kanez al-Oumal 6/153 and Fateh al-Ghadeer 4/456.

[9] Tareekh Baghdad 4/158.

[10] Kanez al-Oumal, 6/392.

[11] The Peak of Eloquence, sermon 5.

2. "And I had been informed of this event and of this time..."[12]

3. "...If you know what I know of the unknown that is kept wrapped up from you, certainly you would have gone out into the open weeping over your deeds."[13]

4. "O brother of Kalb! This is not knowledge of hidden things, these matters have been acquired from him [the Prophet] the one of knowledge."[14]

If some of these texts are part of the knowledge of the unknown (foretelling), other texts are definitely related to the past. And if the Messenger of God (s) informed the Imam (a) of information relating to the future, it is likely that he also informed him about the past.

THE PROPHET'S TRADITIONS

The Prophet's traditions included a lot of diverse historical material, some of which was included in the interpretations and explanations of the Holy Quran while others were included, in part or whole, in the narrations of historical events not mentioned in the Quran.

The Commander of the Faithful Ali (a) was by far the most knowledgeable among all the members of the Prophet's

---

[12] The Peak of Eloquence, sermon 16.

[13] The Peak of Eloquence, sermon 116.

[14] The Peak of Eloquence, sermon 126.

household and his companions of what the Prophet (s) said, did or decided. Ali (a) lived in the Prophet's house since his childhood and he was in that house when the Prophet (a) first received his calling. He was also the first person to believe in him and he did not leave the Prophet's side from that point until his death, except when he had to execute missions assigned to him by the Prophet outside of the city, and even these did not keep him away for too long. From this perspective and from his complete devotion to receiving guidance from the Prophet, combined with his full awareness of the knowledge he was receiving, the Imam was by far the most knowledgeable person of the Prophet's traditions and God's book.

READING

It is believed that Imam Ali (a) read historical documents in Arabic and other languages and dialects in the region where he was active. This was especially after he moved from Hijaz to Iraq, in addition to the issues of governance and sedition that ensued and forced him to travel between Iraq and Syria. However, we do not know if these documents were given to him by chance, or if he searched for such books and read them or were read to him in their original language. We do believe that most probably he knew the literary languages and dialects prevalent at that time and region.

ANCIENT MONUMENTS

It is conceivable that the architectural monuments of ancient nations were among the sources of the historical knowledge for Imam Ali (a). This speculation is largely supported by his saying in the above-mentioned text: "... and I walked in their footsteps..." which is a clear indication that he meant the architectural monuments.

During his lifetime, the Imam (a) became very acquainted with four of Islam's main regions: the Arabian Peninsula, Yemen, Iraq, and Syria.

We believe that he had visited the ruins of ancient civilizations in these countries. And if this had occurred - and we believe it most likely did - it is certain that the Imam (a) did not visit these monuments as a tourist seeking entertainment and culture, or as an archaeologist researching the details of the ruins. Instead he would have visited these sites as a thinker looking for lessons to complement his theoretical knowledge of the fate of those people that passed. He would observe the remains and the ruins of their cities and institutions, which could no longer survive and consequently collapsed.

It is our belief that these are the known, assumed, and probable sources from which Imam Ali (a) derived his historical knowledge.

PREACHING AND GUIDANCE

The Imam (a) used history in three areas: guidance, thought, and politics. The latter two are given greater focus in the second the third parts of this book.

Here, on preaching and guidance, we are faced with an important question:

Why does the Imam (a) incorporate history in his sermons, conversations, speeches and books related to the political and intellectual thinking, as well as in other areas of his guiding role as a visionary and a statesman? Why history?

To answer this question and the doubts about the usefulness of history in the cultural makeup of humans and society, or its characteristic as a contributing factor to intellectual growth, we say:

Human life across all people, places, and time, is the same in its roots, basic components and motivations. It is a flowing river of experiences, hopes, accomplishments and disappointments. The present issues present a reason to study the past as an integral and necessary work in the proper and objective search for answers that are more correct and wiser. That would lead to the right solutions or at least to some of the right solutions for solving the problems humans are facing. These solutions would be based on previous human experiences.

This approach irritates some intellectuals engaged in politics as well as some politicians claiming to be intellectuals. Both of these groups believe that the historicism, or historical rationalism, hinder our growth in the present time and our progress toward the future. They argue that it unnecessarily draws us back to the past, its values and its beliefs. History, in the eyes of these two groups, is a disease that distorts the present and destroys the future.

But this opinion is far from being true.

Though we believe history is an essential component in the cultural structure of humans and society and a supporting element in intellectual development, we do not claim that it is wise for man to make himself a prisoner of history. We do not ascribe to the belief that history is the ultimate truth; rather it is just one step of many towards the development of the empirical truth. This is an exaggerated and excessive intellectual position.

But on the other hand, it is not wise for humans to live in the present and move towards the future without regards to their roots. When people are not conscious of their nation's, let alone humanity's, history they lose their chance at proper perspective. They lose the ability to accurately evaluate situations they face in the present and the challenges they will face in the future. They figuratively isolate themselves in a vacuum.

For these reasons, we believe that a balanced use of history, one characterized by wisdom and moderation, gives us the ability to progress in our present affairs and gives us greater depth for our future. In this case, history deepens our moral sense when we make future decisions that will affect the lives of generations to come. With these decisions we create what would be their present. It would be our future from our current perspective, but we may not see it since we could very well be dead at that time. Thus, they and not we will carry the burden and consequences of our decisions.

Without reviewing the past and what it provides in depth in vision, richness in human experience, and awareness for the continuation of human civilization for us and for future generations, we would not be able to avoid past blunders and mistakes. We would not be able to benefit from the results of the successful experiments of the past. We may also make reckless and dangerous decisions that negatively affect us and the fate of future generations.

Exaggeration in reviewing history, in thoughts and actions, may transform history into a tomb for the present and the future. It could also render a person a stranger in the world where he lives, a world that is teeming with life and progress toward the future all around him.

In addition, excess rejection of history and turning away from its experiences and exploits could render a person like "a feather in the wind" unable to hold on to the present. It could cause him to lose the ability to exercise his principal role in building civilization. Instead he would become a pawn set by others merely reflecting their will, ideas and aspirations.

Therefore, it is a must that humans deal with history in moderation. They must enable the use of history as a guide for their progress, and a tool to reap the fruits of a fertile present for a promising future.

It is in the light of this necessity that the Commander of the Faithful 'Ali ibn Abi Talib (a) dealt with history in the fields of politics, intellectualism, and preaching.

Our main concern in this study is to identify the Imam's historical perspective in the political and intellectual fields. As to the field of preaching and its historical content, we will suffice with analyzing a sermon from the Peak of Eloquence while showcasing its historical perspective.

* * *

In the chapter on *Preaching* in our book *Dirasat fi Nahj Al-Balagha (Studies in the Peak of Eloquence)*[1] we analyzed the sermons of the Commander of the Faithful Ali (a) with respect to the political, social and psychological conditions that specifically dominated Iraqi society during the time of the Imam's rule.

We revealed that the Imam was not preaching an ascetical ideology in his sermons. He does not take a staunchly negative attitude of the worldly life, striving for it or enjoying it. On the contrary, in his sermons and intellectual guidance in general, he called to face life realistically and truthfully, warning of relentlessly pursuing deceptive hopes and false dreams that have no support or basis in reality.

We also revealed that the negative movements of asceticism, particularly from the ages of regression, affected the common perception of the Imam's sermons in the Peak of Eloquence. This movement is alien to Islamic thinking, ethics and laws. Therefore, the perception they produced is wrong and does not represent the Imam's purposes and objectives from his sermons to his community.

The Imam does not call for an ascetical ideology in his sermons with historical context. Rather he addresses a specific issue in his community that seems unaware of their unfortunate fate,

---

[1] Muhammad Mahdi Chamseddine, Studies in Nahj al-Balagha (Third Edition), Beirut

neglectful of their duties in struggling for their own souls and against their enemies, yearning for the pleasures and wealth worthy only of a stable society that has good security and high political and social status and that has eliminated the covetous and conspirators. Such was not the situation in Iraqi society during the rule of the Imam (a). Rather it was a perturbed society suffering from degradation in its external and internal security as well as disarray in its politics. As a result, this fueled the ambitions of the Umayyad rule in Syria and pushed it towards the conspiracy against Iraq.

Below is an example of text from a sermon where history is an essential leading component.

The Imam (a) said:

> *So now, certainly I frighten you from this world for it is sweet and green, surrounded by lusts, and liked for its immediate enjoyments. It excites wonder with small things, is ornamented with (false) hopes and decorated with deception. Its rejoicing does not last and its afflictions cannot be avoided. It is deceitful, harmful, changing, perishable, exhaustible, liable to destruction, eating away and destructive. When it reaches the extremity of desires of those who incline towards it and feel happy with it, the position is just what God, the Glorified, says (in the Qur'an):*

... like the water which send We down from heaven, and the herbage of the earth mingleth with it, then it becometh dry stubble which the winds scatter; for God over all things hath power. (18:45)

No person gets rejoicing from this world but tears come to him after it, and no one gets its comforts in the front but he has to face hardships in the rear. No one receives the light rain of ease in it but the heavy rain of distress pours upon him. It is just worthy of this world that in the morning it supports a man but in the evening it does not recognise him. If one side of it is sweet and pleasant the other side is bitter and distressing.

No one secures enjoyment from its freshness but he has to face hardship from its calamities. No one would pass the evening under the wing of safety but that his morning would be under the feathers of the wing-tip of fear. It is deceitful, and all that is there in it is deception. It is perishable and all that is on it is to perish. There is no good in its provisions except in piety. Whoever takes little from it collects much of what would give him safety, while one who takes much from it takes much of what would ruin him. He would shortly depart from his collection. How many people relied on it but it distressed them; (how many) felt peaceful with it but it tumbled them down; how many were prestigious but it made them low and how many were proud but it made them disgraceful.

Its authority is changing. Its life is dirty. Its sweet water is bitter. Its sweetness is like myrrh. Its foods are poisons. Its means are weak. The living in it is exposed to death; the healthy in it is exposed to disease. Its realm is (liable to be) snatched away. The strong in it is (liable to be) defeated and the rich is (liable to be) afflicted with misfortune. The neighbour in it is (liable to be) plundered.

Are you not (residing) in the houses of those before you, who were of longer ages, better traces, had bigger desires, were more in numbers and had greater armies. How they devoted themselves to the world and how they showed preference to it! Then they left it without any provision that could convey them through, or the back (of a beast for riding) to carry them.

Did you get the news that the world was ever generous enough to present ransom for them, or gave them any support or afforded them good company? It rather inflicted them with troubles, made them languid with calamities, molested them with catastrophes, threw them down on their noses, trampled them under hoofs and helped the vicissitudes of time against them. You have observed its strangeness towards those who went near it, acquired it and appropriated it, till they depart from it for good. Did it give them any provision other than starvation or make them stay in other than narrow places, or give them light other than gloom, or give them in the end anything other than repentance? Is this what you much ask for or remain satisfied with, or towards which you feel greedy? How bad is this abode for him who did not suspect it (to be so) and did not entertain fear from it?

You should know as you do know, that you have to leave it and depart from it. While in it, take lesson from those "who proclaimed 'who is more powerful than we'" (Qur'an , 41 :15) but they were carried to their graves, though not as riders. They were then made to stay in the graves, but not as guests. Graves were made for them from the surface of the ground. Their shrouds were made from earth....

They have exchanged the back (surface) of the earth with its stomach (interior), vastness with narrowness, family with loneliness, and light with darkness....[2]

* * *

In this sermon, the Imam (a) focused, as he did in most of his sermons, on two permanent factors related to the nature of life on earth:

---

[2] The Peak of Eloquence, sermon 111.

The factor of change and unsteadiness of life. Life is a movement and a system of interaction. It is a group of forces and energies interacting to complement or compete with one another within the grand universe. Being all of this, life is unsteady, ever-changing, and constantly transforming. It is in a permanent state of becoming and does not settle on one condition nor does it keep the same pattern.

The time factor. The effect of time on things is apparent to all people with insight. Time is constantly disintegrating life. From the moment life is born in something or something begins to exist, be it living or non-living, its presence starts to melt, disintegrate and die. Life is born with time but time is constantly killing life.

These two factors, change and time, are not specific to the human world alone, they affect everything and prevent stability for everything: inanimate objects, plants, animals, and humans. With regards to these two factors, only humans differ in that they are given intellect and perception so they are able to understand the tragic impact of these factors on life and existence.

Humans' awareness of these two factors and their impact on living and non-living things equips them to face life and its temporary pleasures, generous promises, and bright hopes with a clear mind that is free of illusions. It enhances the realistic tendency in approaching life and dealing with the world. This tendency that makes hopes less glamorous, attractive and alluring and makes triumphs less a source of pride and arrogance, and makes tragedies less painful. It also enhances the immunity of humans in the fierce struggle against the adversities of time, disappointments and lost efforts, and the disastrous occurrence of disease and death... It is so they do not fall apart for any reason nor do they give up, surrender or run away from work. Rather, they become driven to work and struggle for themselves, their families, communities and world all over again because they are not surprised by disappointments and failures. Instead they had prepared themselves to accept them and therefore they were prepared to overcome them, and resume work again with renewed and realistic sense of hope.

Overall, the awareness of humans of these two factors is essential in having a realistic outlook. Their awareness of their profound and fateful impact on their own lives and the lives of others helps them cope with life in all its facets. With all the good and the ugly, pain and pleasure, reality and imagination, and success and failure, human beings can see the potential in themselves and the reality that shapes their purpose.

When the Imam (a) includes the historical element in his sermons and talks about the people of the past, what befell them from disasters and pain and how their lives changed from a radiant greatness to extinction, he is offering a theoretical analysis relevant to the reality of the lives of his contemporaries. He is providing practical examples of the lives of other peoples... He is offering his contemporaries the experience of others as they know it and as they witness its remaining evidence where they live.

People who were moved by the adversities of life built these cities and abodes, these towns and farms, and these castles and forts in previous eras. They were moved by life's joys and sorrows, its disappointments and the hopes for the things they were to accomplish. Then they died and were separated from all that filled their lives with dreams and wishes, aspirations and ambitions, love and hatred, and friendships and enmities...

They had longer lifetimes, they were more powerful... "and [were] larger in numbers" and they had dedicated all their abilities, intelligence and knowledge to this world. They planned for it and prepared themselves to face it and they were not distracted by considerations of or work for life in the Hereafter. But all this preparation did not benefit them because the factors of change, unsteadiness, and time are always at work. They are still working today and will work in the future to fragment the lives of those people. Life was, as it is today and as it will remain in the future, holding at its core and in its depths during its birth, growth and prosperity, the seeds of its contraction, withering and eventual death.

* * *

Imam Ali (a) introduces the element of history in his sermons because it enlightens the present by adding the experiences of the past. He thereby enriches us and makes us better equipped to face the present with a realistic attitude and a mind free of illusions. This is so humans do not waver or give up in the face of adversity, become oppressors, or be overcome with pride at when reaching success.

PART II

HISTORY AND THOUGHT

INTRODUCTION

The Imam utilized history in the field of thought just as he used it in the field of politics.

He was a man with a mission and that mission was Islam. This mission encompasses life in its entirety: organization, legislation and processes. It is universal in its nature and extends until the end of time. God wanted it to be the religion of man leading him towards excellence through achieving balance and advancement.

It is a mission based on science and knowledge and it rejects ignorance. Islam rejects ignorance because it enfranchises its enemies to sneak under the cover of ignorance's darkness into the hearts and minds of its believing followers. In turn, they twist and distort its beliefs, legislations and processes. Then they mislead the people by presenting the truth as falsehood and what is right as wrong.

Hence this was one of the biggest concerns for this man on a mission. There was emphasis on a continuous preparedness to make Muslims fully knowledgeable of Islam. The Muslim ought to be in a state of renewed awareness and growth to the truth of Islam, its essence, its processes and its goals. This is so the Muslim enlightened with knowledge is immune to the confusion and misinformation that comes his way. Instead, he is confident of his path. Islam is immune to distortion and deviation and every Muslim becomes a well-informed guard of his faith, which is the essential meaning and honor for his existence.

From this perspective, Imam Ali (a) was continuously teaching his community and companions. Imam Ali's (a) companions were scholars spreading their knowledge and enlightenment among the people through dialogue, speeches, teaching and instructional circles.

The Imam (a) used to choose people with insight[1] as his governors and representatives to the various towns. These people had knowledge, awareness and firm beliefs in their faith

---

[1] People with insight is an Islamic expression dating back to the beginning of Islam. It means the enlightened believers who make their political and other decisions based on convictions inspired by the Islamic ideology, not connected to opportunistic considerations. It is certain that early on, this expression became an Islamic cultural term that indicates the category of people who are aware of Islam in its proper form and who are committed to it in their lives in an accurate manner. These people take principled approaches to social and political problems that they face in life and in society. They do not listen to personal or tribal considerations, nor do they stand by in the face of these problems. Rather they demonstrate their theoretical commitment through their daily struggle against deviations.

Review the detailed research on this topic in our book "Ansar al-Hussein: al-Reejal wa al-Dalalat" – first edition- Dar elFikr – 1395 AH, 1975 AD, chapter of "Al-Nokhbah" Pages 165-170.

so they became teachers and mission-oriented men. This was all in addition to their administrative duties. The Imam (a) would guide them towards this educational and guidance role. An example of this was what he wrote to Qutham ibn Abbas, his governor in Mecca:

So now, you should make all the necessary arrangements for the people for the pilgrimage of Hajj and remind people of the importance of the Days of God[2] and hold meetings for them in the mornings and evenings so you guide those with questions, teach the ignorant and remind the knowledgeable.[3]

* * *

The Imam (a) used history in his intellectual discourse to give warmth, vitality and impact to the mind and to give it depth in time and human experience. He thereby made intellectual matters a part of daily life that carries within its folds the taste of the human suffering.

* * *

Reasoning is contemplation and thought is derived from contemplation. According to [Arabic] linguists, thought has two meanings:

---

[2] The Days of God is an Islamic cultural term predominantly used to denote the major disasters that befell nations and communities as a result of their deviation from the ideology, laws and ethics. It can be used to denote the major victories achieved by believers who changed the course of history or the history of a believing group or people.

[3] The Peak of Eloquence, Chapter al-Ketab, number 67.

* First: Thought is the power residing within the brain, the center of thinking. We do however have to recognize that other parts of the body impact our ability to think in terms of health and sickness impacting the process of thinking. In this sense, thought is the instrument for thinking.

* Second: The impact of thinking. Such impact leads to the order of things in the mind from which new knowledge is generated or existing knowledge is deepened and expanded. Thought in this sense describes the act of thinking or the thinking process. This is the explanation of the meaning of and clarification of the words thought and thinking linguistically.

* There is a third meaning for the word thought and it has been the dominant understanding in the contemporary. Perhaps it had entered the Arabic vernacular through European uses. It is the ideas and information that the result of thinking or thoughts (the first meaning above) make the subject of its work (the second meaning above). For example, it is said Islamic thought, Christian thought, Marxist thought, religious thought, or materialistic thought.... This is intended to mean the ideas, approaches and information that form and make up a doctrine, philosophy or religion.

Our research in this work targets the third meaning above for the word.

Thought in the culture that makes up the character of every nation is in two parts: living thought and dead thought. The first one is used to indicate thought in our present time and the second is what we, in our present time, call heritage.

* * *

The origin of heritage [in the Arabic language] is from inheritance. And the word heritage is mentioned one time in the Holy Quran when God addresses the infidels saying: "... And you eat away the heritage, devouring (everything) indiscriminately..."[4]

The word inheritance in Arabic is used to indicate materialism and intangibles and that use has many clear examples. However, its use to indicate materialism, in particular, in the Quran occurred in multiple places:

1. *Then there came after them an evil posterity who inherited the Book, taking only the frail good of this low life and saying: It will be forgiven us...*[5]

2. *Then We gave the Book for an inheritance to those whom We chose from among Our servants; but of them is he who makes his soul to suffer a loss, and of them is he who takes a*

---

[4] The Holy Quran, 89:19.
[5] The Holy Quran, 7:169.

middle course, and of them is he who is foremost in deeds of goodness by God's permission...[6]

3. *... And those who were made to inherit the Book after them are most surely in disquieting doubt concerning it.[7]*

This word was also used in the prophetic traditions with the meaning of intangibles. It is narrated that Imam Al-Sadiq (a) relates from the Prophet (s):

... Scholars are the heirs of prophets. The prophets did not leave behind dinars or dirhams but rather they left science as their inheritance so whoever takes from it, takes plenty of it.[8]

The subject of inheritance was mentioned multiple times in The Peak of Eloquence in different topics, both in the past and present tenses as a verb and to indicate both materialism and intangibles as a noun. Among its uses to indicate intangibles, the Imam said, "no inheritance like refinement ..."[9] and "...Knowledge is a venerable estate..."[10] He also used it in regards to intangibles as related to political influence when he said, "The Umayyads are allowing me the inheritance of

---

[6] The Holy Quran, 35:32.

[7] The Holy Quran, 42:14.

[8] Mohamad bin Ya'coub al-Kaleenee: Al-Kafee, volume 1, page 34.

[9] The Peak of Eloquence, Selections of Sayings and Preachings, topic of Governance, number 54 and 113.

[10] The Peak of Eloquence, Selections of Sayings and Preachings, topic of Governance, number 5.

Muhammad (s) bit by bit..."[11] and "...So I adopted patience although there was pricking in the eye... I watched the plundering of my inheritance..."[12]

* * *

In light of these uses, it can be said that heritage or inheritance is, in the general and not in the nomenclatorial sense, all that is left behind in life, be it materialistic or intangible, by one person to another who comes after him in time, regardless how far apart they are.

And so, what we call heritage or inheritance is not something that was in the possession of the heir but rather it came to him from someone else. He may or may not be in need of it. If he needs it, he may realize that need and use it and be benefitted by it. He may realize that need but for one reason or another, turn away from it. Or he may not realize his need of it and ignore it or discard it except as it is considered a relic that connects him to his loved ones and predecessors – that would give it a sentimental but not a practical value in the heir's life.

This means that heritage or inheritance is not necessarily an essential ingredient in present life. It does not represent an component without which the present would be spoiled because it occupies such an essential part in it or fulfills an

---

[11] The Peak of Eloquence, Sermon 77.

[12] The Peak of Eloquence, Sermon 5.

urgent and indispensable need. Rather, it may be, in the eyes of the heir, something merely to acquire and use but losing it does not change the present or make it lacking. The heritage may have no more than an emotional value in the eyes of the heir and losing it would have no other impact otherwise. It might even be a burden, in the eyes of the heir, or an impediment to his growth and prosperity and as such, he strives to discard it and get rid of it and its effects.

This is an analysis of the concept of inheritance or heritage [as understood] in the Arabic language, in the general and not in the idiosyncratic sense.

In recent times, the word heritage has been used in the Arabic language by researchers, writers and scholars to indicate the impact of Islamic thought in various fields. These fields include jurisprudence, the principles of jurisprudence, history, literature, philosophy, and other intellectual areas by Muslims in the Arabic language.

Such is thought and such is heritage.

* * *

Thought, in the present concepts of civilization, is therefore the information, laws, values and practices that make up the cultural and civilized character of a nation, distinguishing it from other nations and determining its role in the impact of history.

These laws, values, practices and information are a nation's mind, soul and conscience. It views the world, life, humans and other nations through the lens of its information, laws, values and practices. It faces its problems and life issues with the solutions and positions that are nurtured by this thought. Its entire theoretical and intellectual product is characterized by this thought, encompassed in its spirits, and guided by its light.

For example: Marxism is the thought of the Communist world. It constitutes the mind, soul and conscience of its people and distinguishes them from those in the capitalist world by the characteristics it has on their way of life. Furthermore, it also characterizes their cultural and theoretical output with the distinguishing marks of Marxism. In fact, the soviet theorists aspire to imprint scientific theories with the characteristics of Marxism. This is in present time.

Christianity, in the eyes of Europe, had similar characteristics before and in the Middle Ages, as did Communism in the eyes of China, Hinduism in the eyes of India, Zoroastrian in the eyes of Iran, and Islam in the eyes of the Muslim world since its advent and to this day.

Each school of thought has a core on which it falls back as a measure of resonance, authenticity and integrity. This core is the basis of everything since it is the biggest asset in the cultural make up of a nation.

For example, the book *Capital* for Marxism and Communism, the *Torah* and *Bible* for Christianity, *Bhagavad Gita* for Hinduism, the *Quran* for Islam, and *Avesta* for Zoroastrianism... As such, every school of thought has a center of thoughts that outlines its major philosophies and principles.

This is the concept of thought from the present cultural perspective.

* * *

Heritage in the modern understanding is merely culture and theoretical knowledge and, in most cases, does not reach the level of thought that we explained above. We can say that heritage is dead thought.

Heritage does not enter into the heart of a nation's culture, feed its practical mind, or has impact on effectiveness and progress over the course of history. It does not add value to its existence, guide its path in life or distinguish it from other nations. In general, all that is positive in thought for a nation is different from heritage. Heritage is the remnants from forefathers and while it was suitable for that past life with its methods and styles, it is not suitable for the most part or in its entirety for present life. We keep it in our lives, study it and built institutions for it not so we can build our lives on it or define our nation's character but rather because we have emotional ties to it or because it represents an important link in the history of our growth. It has sentimental and academic (theoretical) but not practical value, at least for the most part. We study it, verify it, publish it and keep it so we can know how we were and not how we will be and so we can see an illustration of our past and not to draw out our future. In the best of cases, heritage is something from the heart and emotions and not something from the mind or deeds.

That is concept of heritage in the present cultural perspective.

* * *

Here I would like to raise a very serious issue, one of great importance for us Muslims in the present day. It is that the vast majority of Muslims, who are educated and cultured according to Western ways and methods, see Islam, with all of its culture, organization and civilization, not as thought but as dead thought.

Praise be to God and His grace, the overall vast majority of Muslims still deal with Islam as their thought, not merely their heritage, and they are keen to the best of their ability to establish their lives according to the guidance of its provisions and values. We do have to recognize however that modern life frequently compels many of them to violate some of the religion's rules or it tempts them to violate those rules because it is a life that is not based on Islam and it derives its intellectual, moral, aesthetic and practical concepts from sources other than Islam. But this vast majority still considers Islam to be its thought as we said above. They do even when they breach its rules, whether out of necessity or carelessness, in the major or minor affairs of their lives. Islam is their belief, their laws[13] and their values.

We now circle back, after this tangent, to explaining the position of Muslims who treat Islam as their heritage and not their thought.

They perceive Islam, not the doctrine but the laws and values, as the thoughts of a bygone era and that in present day, it is only heritage by comparison to our modern life and its legislation and values. It is only heritage and it represents an earlier stage in our growth and our evolution in time. As such, we cannot consider it as our thought, instead it is our heritage and a source of pride for us. It is the object of our love and appreciation but it is not fit for shaping our lives or be the infrastructure upon which we build our paths or derive our values.

Modern Arab intellectuals, who are concerned with the issues of the Arab renaissance, often use the word heritage[14] to

---

[13] It is important to note that the laws of Islam urge Muslims' conduct to be in respect and observation of the law of the land they live in. There should be no contradiction between respecting and abiding by the law of the land while observing the laws of the faith. – Eds.

[14] Here we point out that some publishing houses in some of the Arabic countries, some of which are part of official cultural institutions, have published books on Islamic thought under the title of "our heritage" or "heritage series" among other such titles. We note here that not all those who use the word heritage about Islamic thought have that perspective about that school of thought. Some Muslim intellectuals and researches who are faithful to the religion, have used the word heritage about Islamic

express one topic or another of Islamic thought. They maintain that this Islamic heritage is not for our present day nor is it for the Arabs of present day, but rather it is that of our Arab ancestors and we just inherited it from them. They ascertain that it is not beneficial for us to take it in its entirety and emulate it in our approach and laws for our lives because it is an impediment for growth and prosperity for this life. So do we reject it all? Do we preserve it as a relic from our history? Do we subject this heritage to some selection measures that are consistent with our present life and contemporary thoughts and refuse the rest of this heritage that does not agree, or may even contradict, our present day thinking? These intellectuals are committing a fatal error in this important, and rather fateful, issue, not just for Arabs themselves but also for all Muslims.

Islam remains today the "thought" for Muslims, including the Arabs among them, and will remain the school of thought for all Muslims. It did not become "heritage" in need of "revival" by reaching a degree of atrophy, shrinkage, irrelevance or forgetfulness in the hearts and minds of Muslims like the one experienced in Europe, necessitating the Renaissance for the Greek Roman heritage.

Islam remains "alive" and full of vitality in the hearts and minds of Muslims and it is still capable of "moving" hundreds of

---

thought without intending an intellectual position from that school of thought as that word means in present day but rather they intended the linguistic significance.

millions of Muslims across the world into action and towards its great noble goals. Therefore, it remains the "thought" for these hundreds of millions of people. It does not "move" them because of the presence of foreign and oppressing paralytic constraints for Muslims in their own religion. These are foreign materialistic forces that have colonized the Muslim world and kept Islam from leading and took its place at the helm.

Therefore, Islam is not dead "heritage" or legacy whereby we are disagreeing about whether or not to "revive" it or to revive parts of that would befit modern times. It is alive and well and what some are calling for us to do is to "kill this alive thought" so they can replace it with a strange school of thought that is a modern materialistic one.

These modern materialistic forces have not succeeded in "killing Islam" for it is still alive and well, as we have discussed. But they have succeeded in imposing themselves on the lives of Muslims who still carry in their hearts and minds an Islam that is very much alive and capable of impact. Though such forces may forbid them from making an impact, they are unable to suppress such capability.

The continuation of efforts by our intellectuals, who are impacted by this materialistic culture, to impose it on the actual lives of Muslims and isolate Islam from modern day life will not lead to "killing Islam" just like it will not lead to "liberating" Muslims or Arabs. It will however lead to more internal disruption and cultural crises to humans who are divided amongst themselves and who are torn between everyday necessities on one hand and their intellectual, psychological, moral and emotional convictions on the other hand. This will lead, as it already has in the entire Muslim world including the Arabic portion of it, to the loss of effectiveness and ability to adapt when facing life's challenges. This will in turn lead to further underdevelopment and inability to keep up with the progress of other nations. By doing so, these intellectuals are doing harm when they believe they are helping. Instead of providing Arabs the opportunity to overcome difficulties and challenging factors, they are adding another reason for backwardness, one that exacerbates the situation because it is presented under the guise of progress. As such, the condition of the Arabs in this case is not unlike a cat that licks a grater which tempts its tongue but makes it bleed and the cat thinks it is feeding itself from that grater when the latter is only tempting it in reality.

* * *

We saw it fit that we present our research on history in the field of thought from Imam Ali's (a) perspective with this introduction because of

* Our strong feelings about the seriousness of this issue;

* The issue of our position on Islamic thought and

* The necessity of correcting the prevailing perception of this thought that is behind our entire existence.

PROPHETHOOD

THE BEGINNING OF THE ERA OF MAN

It would seem to us from the words of Ali (a) that the historical era of man began when prophets appeared in human society. These prophets lead their communities towards a better life and a more complete human existence.

Prehistoric times then for humanity are the ones prior to prophets when humans lived in a state of primitive innocence. The human soul was still naïve and devoid of learning... As such, humanity, in this definition of prehistoric times, did not have experiences and struggles which could provide educational or cultural benefits to a fully developed civilized society with a high degree of complexity, presumably built based on the guidance of the conclusive message and the finest of prophets and that is the Islam world.

For the above reasons, we do not find in all of the Imam's words anything addressing the times before the prophets and as such, we conclude that he considers the emergence of prophethood and prophets in human society the beginning of the historical era for mankind.

God Almighty indicates the beginning of the time of the prophets in human society when he said in the Holy Quran:

> *(All) people are a single nation; so God raised prophets as bearers of good news and as warners, and He revealed with them the Book with truth, that it might judge between people in that in which they differed; and none but the very people who were given it differed about it after clear arguments had come to them, revolting among themselves; so God has guided by His will those who believe to the truth about which they differed and God guides whom He pleases to the right path.*[1]

"(All) people are a single nation." In the time before the prophets, prehistoric man lived in one primitive community based on unity of interests and blood on the one hand, and the negative factors of the simplicity of and inaction in life at the time on the other. This simplicity was a product of the uncomplicated needs and the availability of the means to meet

---

[1] The Holy Quran, 2:213.

those needs in nature without the necessity of conflict and power struggle.

However the ever-developing movement of life, the growing number of the members of the species, and the varying mental and physical capacities along with such other similar divisive and complex factors led to the emergence of conflict within the various developing human groups as well as conflict and infighting among their members and classes. Perhaps the first display of this was the first crime among the sons of Adam when one of them killed his brother. God tells us the story of that incident in the Holy Quran.[2] Our hesitation in labeling this incident as the first crime stems from the possibility that the "Quranic" Adam does not represent the beginning of humankind on Earth but rather he represents the beginning of the human species as it exists today. The latter possibility would mean that there was a human race whose beginning was marked by an Adam predating the "Quranic" Adam. Only God knows. In that case, verse 213 of the chapter of the Cow in the Holy Quran would be chronicling a period in the human race prior to the one that began with the "Quranic" Adam.

At any rate, at this stage in human development, the unity in blood was no longer sufficient to lead to unity in the community. Interests were no longer common or aligned and the human soul no longer virgin, primitive or naïve. Under

---

[2] The Holy Quran, 5:27-31.

such circumstances, it became impossible for the human race to grow based on instincts alone, without any resource to help it with perspective or conflict resolution. At this stage in human development, God's mercy and wisdom decreed that He send prophets who would provide humans with guidance to help them exit the time of instinct and enter the time of intellect, and from the time of conflict driven by instinct and strength to the logic of order and the guidance of laws.

With the onset of the times of the prophets, humans achieved a great and decisive leap forward in their evolution to higher levels and their growth. Human society, through the impact of prophethood, grew from being an animalistic biological being to become a mental and spiritual phenomenon. Prophethood provided human society with intellect and spirit.

Prophethood achieved for humans a finer unity than the unity of blood and biology it previously enjoyed before the times of conflict, division and infighting. This unity has a basis of belief and as such, human relations evolved higher, from materialistic relations to ones with meaning. The era of prophets launched the era of man.

After providing historic perspective for this phase, the Quranic verse goes on to say that the ensuing conflict among humans, after the start of the times of prophets, became conflicts in interpretation, religions and beliefs. Reasons for conflict and oppression among people and exploitation of the weak by the strong were not abolished with the arrival of the prophets; rather they continued and became more varied. However, they were not manifestations of instincts but rather of the law. If it were impossible for the human race to find a stable basis for unity and cooperation based on instinct and material relations, it is in fact possible for it to find such a stable basis for unity, cooperation and excellence based on law. This would be in addition to the significance of religion and the enrichment it provides in the spirit and morality of humans. This is a result of humans exchanging materialistic relations with meaningful ones. The fact that humans have not attained such a state since the time of the prophets is not a reflection of the absence of the necessary means; rather it is because of the poor choices humans have made and because of the misuse of the available freedoms.

We elaborated in the discussion about some aspects of the verse to shed light on the idea expressed by the Imam (as) in relationship to prophethood and the beginning of the historical era of humans. He said:

> From his (Adam's) progeny God chose prophets and took their pledge for his revelation and for carrying His message as their trust. In course of time many people perverted God's trust with them and ignored His position and took compeers along with Him. Satan turned them away from knowing Him and kept them aloof from His worship. Then God sent His Messengers and series of His

prophets towards them.... God never allowed His creation to remain without a Prophet deputized by Him, or a book sent down from Him or a binding argument or a standing plea. These Messengers were such that they did not feel little because of smallness of their number or of largeness of the number of their falsifiers. Among them was either a predecessor who would name the one to follow or the follower who had been introduced by the predecessor. In this way ages passed by and times rolled on, fathers passed away while sons took their places...[3]

The Imam expresses various aspects from that holy verse. God's mercy, wisdom and grace had Him send the prophets to enlighten people's minds and to elevate society from the mere materialistic and biological relations they had to relations with meaning and law. This need was a result of human life becoming more complex given the development of society and the intricacy of relationships therein. This in turn led to conflict between the cooperation mandated by life in a community and the monopolization characteristic of instinct and individual spirit. This was also accompanied by deviation from the straightforward and simple needs of instinct, albeit naïve at that time, to recognize the Almighty Creator.

* * *

---

[3] The Peak of Eloquence, Sermon 1.

The existence of prophets was frequent throughout the mankind's history: to enlighten their minds, formulate their concepts, improve their lives and set them gently on the path to excellence... The impact of prophets was progressive in a manner ascending towards greater excellence, and the more complete and beautiful, responding at each stage of human history to the needs of that stage and spreading in it the seeds for further growth in the future so it reaches further growth and perfection... The culmination of prophethood was reached with the final and uniting message; that of the Seal of the Prophets, Prophet Muhammad, peace be upon him and his progeny.

Imam Ali (a) would say,

> *Until God deputized Muhammad (peace be upon him and his progeny) as His Prophet, in fulfilment of His promise and in completion of His Prophethood. His pledge had been taken from the Prophets, his traits of character were well reputed and his birth was honorable...[4]*

He said in another sermon:

> *But He provided to them the proofs through His chosen Messengers and bearers of the trust of His Message, age after age till the process came to end with our Prophet*

---

[4] The Peak of Eloquence, Sermon 1.

Muhammad - God may bless him and his descendants -
and His pleas and warnings reached finality.[5]

THE FUNCTION OF PROPHETHOOD

What is the function of prophethood in human society?

As we understand from the words of the Commander of the Faithful, the function of prophethood can be summed up in two major areas:

* First, and most importantly, its function is to revive the pure and upright human instinct. This instinct guides humans to the true faith in God Almighty and makes them aware that they are one of His creations and helps them realize their position in this universe. This true and enlightened belief is contingent upon correcting the human path towards excellence by making his impact on history better connected to the doctrine of monotheism and its implications.

* Second, and in some ways it is the result of the first, its function is to configure the spiritual, psychological and social incentives to complete the process of mental, physical and social progress in life in a manner that ensures balance between the spiritual and moral growth and

---

[5] The Peak of Eloquence, Sermon 91.

physical growth. Religion is the balance between human development and its activities.

This is the function of prophethood as understood from the Holy Quran and the noble traditions.

A prophet guides the people from darkness to the light. From creed and theology to social and political life, he provides his people that guidance. He corrects their views about their place in the universe. He then helps the good humans who strive towards perfection to achieve the balanced spiritual and material progress in both form and content.

A prophet is not a great inventor or a great planner who masters machinery or institutions, nor is prophethood a center for research and studies and the like.

The human mind is the one that invents machinery, establishes institutions and devises plans after the proper incentives for growth and development become available. When the proper incentives are combined with the spiritual and moral values, humans arrive at organizational and material achievements consistent with the requirements of the faith. Thus, they are able to provide man with a happy and good life and with God's blessings and mercy in the afterlife. When spiritual and moral values are not combined with the incentives for growth and development in the material world, man will achieve organizational and materialistic goals that provide him with strength, pleasure and prosperity without providing him happiness or a wholesome life.

* * *

Our understanding of the function of prophethood, as reflected in the texts in the Peak of Eloquence, is derived from the texts where the Imam describes the state of the world on the eve of the start of Prophet Mohamad's mission. This is because texts describing prophets before Prophet Muhammad are rare on the one hand and on the other hand, resemble signals for the most part, dominated by overall views.

However this does not impact our understanding of the function of prophethood for it is the same message from the dawn of human history to its culmination with the prophethood of Muhammad and the message of Islam. There are no significant differences in the role of prophethood in terms of primary functions. The only main difference is in the degree of inclusiveness and breadth of coverage of religious laws, as they relate to human activities and to general messages to other people.

* * *

He said (a):

> .... *Then God sent His Messengers and series of His prophets towards them to get them to fulfil the pledges of His creation, to recall to them His bounties, to exhort*

them by preaching, to unveil before them the hidden virtues of wisdom and show them the signs of His Omnipotence namely the sky which is raised over them, the earth that is placed beneath them, means of living that sustain them, deaths that make them die, ailments that turn them old and incidents that successively betake them...⁶

This text, that provided timing context for past prophets, presented the following issues related to the purpose of sending forth prophets:

COVENANT OF THE INNATE

This relates to the topic of faith and belief in God Almighty and all that follows from that faith in basic issues related to the affairs of life.

Here and in other instances in his lectures and directives, the Imam (a) expressed one of major facts from the Quran, a fact that was directly and indirectly stated in a number of verses, including:

And when your Lord brought forth from the children of Adam, from their backs, their descendants, and made them bear witness against their own souls: Am I not your Lord? They said: Yes! we bear witness. Lest you should say on the day of resurrection: Surely we were heedless of

---

⁶ The Peak of Eloquence, Sermon 1.

this. Or you should say: Only our fathers associated others (with God) before, and we were an offspring after them: Wilt Thou then destroy us for what the vain doers did?[7]

This major issue of faith was repeatedly mentioned in all texts where the Imam (a) discussed the history of prophethood.

AWAKENING THE DEPTH OF MINDS

This relates to bringing forth the mental and psychological strengths in humans to achieve proper progress and positive change in society through the underlying proper historical consciousness.

USING NATURE IN RESEARCH AND PERSPECTIVE

This is illustrated by his words, *"... And show them the signs of His Omnipotence..."*

This issue serves the first two issues above in that observing nature in order to understand it, interact with it and discover it strengthens the faith because nature provides more empirical evidence to divinity issues realized through common sense. Dealing with nature directly also aids in achieving progress and is in fact a primary requisite to achieve material progress. When the issue of faith in the human soul is in concert with his historical impact on nature and society, then his progress is enlightened by faith and the ethics of his soul and mind. His

---

[7] The Holy Quran, 7:172-173.

faith would be one that responds to life on Earth rather than one with a position of hostility and rejection.

* * *

In another text where the Imam chronicled for the world the mission of Prophet Muhammad, he said:

> ... *Until God deputized Muhammad (peace be upon him and his progeny) as His Prophet... The people of the earth at this time were divided in different parties, their aims were separate and ways were diverse. They either likened God with His creation or twisted His Names or turned to else than Him. Through Muhammad (S) God guided them out of wrong and with his efforts took them out of ignorance....[8]*

And he said in another text:

> *God sent the Prophet at a time when the people were going astray in perplexity and were moving here and there in mischief. Desires had deflected them and self-conceit had swerved them. Extreme ignorance had made them foolish. They were confounded by the unsteadiness of matters and the evils of ignorance. Then the Prophet – blessing of God be upon him and his descendants – did his best in giving them sincere advice, himself trod on the*

---

[8] The Peak of Eloquence, Sermon 1.

right path and called (them) towards wisdom and good counsel.[9]

In a third text, the Imam said:

I also stand witness that Muhammad (S) is His slave and His Prophet. God sent him with the illustrious religion... At that time people had fallen in vices whereby the rope of religion had been broken, the pillars of belief had been shaken, principles had been sacrileged, system had become topsy turvy, openings were narrow, passage was dark, guidance was unknown and darkness prevailed. God was being disobeyed, Satan was given support and Belief had been forsaken. As a result the pillars of religion fell down, its traces could not be discerned, its passages had been destroyed and its streets had fallen into decay. People obeyed Satan and treaded his paths. They sought water from his watering places. Through them Satan's emblems got flying and his standard was raised in vices which trampled the people under their hoofs, and treaded upon them with their feet. The vices stood on their toes (in full stature) and the people immersed in them were strayed, perplexed, ignorant and seduced...[10]

---

[9] The Peak of Eloquence, Sermon 95.
[10] The Peak of Eloquence, Sermon 2.

The Imam delineates in these texts the many faces of corruption that was afflicting the world on the eve of the Prophet's mission. These are the major faces of corruption of every age and in every nation. The mission of prophethood, since it emerged and until its culmination with Prophet Muhammad, has been to correct this corruption.

First: Delusion in faith, *"when the people were going astray in perplexity... and were moving here and there in mischief..."* They were perplexed because when man does not settle on a belief, or when general corruption leads him to a worthless doctrine, he feels lost and aimless, without a goal... Having no meaning to his existence. He is overcome with a feeling of futility when he asks himself: Who am I? Why am I here? What is the meaning of my existence? And so goes forth this lost human trying to find an answer where one does not exist because, *"...They either likened God with His creation or twisted His Names or turned to else than Him."*

Second: Political and social corruption: The people's unwarranted vanity made them fall into transgressions and led to degeneration in civilization. It led the strong among them to despise their weak and their poor... and the elite to disparage the rest of the people. Human dignity was taken lightly and the measure of dignity became subject to non-humanitarian factors such as wealth, power, lineage and so forth. As a result, people organized into rival groupings, to each its own belief and path, preference and approach, doctrine and objective. Each fascinated by its own opinion, taken by its own preferences and acting on its own whims.

Prophethood deals with all faces of corruption found in individuals and society, both spiritual and physical. It does this through institutions built to achieve the greater noble end of forming a perfect human.

Throughout history, all prophets had declared this goal, each in his own environment and time, until prophethood was sealed with Muhammad (s). Then the great goal was commensurate with the extent of the concluding message in time and place for all of humanity and for the entire future until the end of time.

> *Then the Prophet – blessing of God be upon him and his descendants – did his best in giving them sincere advice, himself trod on the right path and called (them) towards wisdom and good counsel...*
> *Through Muhammad (s) God guided them out of wrong and with his efforts took them out of ignorance.*

The great noble efforts and the struggles of the prophets were fruitful for their followers in achieving the great goal of setting the human race on the path to excellence. Perhaps this statement causes surprise, wonder and questioning:

How did the venerated prophets achieve this goal when only a few believed in them while the majority of people turned away, and in fact, fought them and rejected them? The goal of prophethood was achieved in every era and during the time of every prophet in two ways:

Firstly, those who believed in the prophet, his message and guidance adhered in their private and public life to the doctrine and its laws that were included in the prophet's message.

Secondly, the goal attained is illustrated in the cultural and spiritual environments that spread in the community as a result of the prophetic message and its followers. The prophetic message also resulted in intellectual and social discussions in the community. Without doubt, this cultural environment left its mark on the concepts, institutions, values and convictions prevalent in society and unconsciously pushed them towards change. This led society towards a better state in its relationships, values, institutions and motivations even when this society for the most part did not believe in the prophet's message.

Hence, the prophets, peace be upon them all, were the fathers of human culture and civilization. The prophets were behind every positive impact experienced and enjoyed by humanity in intellect, tastes, values, institutions and motivations that led to material advancement. Throughout history, and through divine revelation, prophets breathed new life in every society. They brought life that shined like light and a renewed health of enlightenment. They brightened the dark corners and touched the areas of desperation and illness within. Still, the impact had varying degrees. This variance in impact was commensurate with the level of resistance by forces of darkness when they realized the degree of positive influence from the prophets. It was also impacted by the ability of this positive influence to endure when those in power became less attentive or motivated by self-interest.

Thus, it is from this perspective that we believe that every prophet from God was able to guide the people and save them from ignorance. They truly are, peace be upon them all, the great fathers of humanity and civilization.

* * *

The following is another quote from the Imam where he highlights yet another side of the function of prophethood in light of its two great goals; he said:

> Hearts of virtuous persons have been inclined towards him and the reins of eyes have been turned towards him. Through him God buried mutual rancour and put off the flames of revolt. Through him He gave them affection like brothers and separated those who were together (through unbelief). Through him He gave honour to the low and degraded honour (of unbelief).[11]

In this quote, the Imam reveals the ability of prophethood in changing prevailing values in society; these values that govern

---

[11] The Peak of Eloquence, Sermon 96.

and guide relationships between groups and individuals within society. Prophethood replaces these values with others that are consistent with the nature of a prophetic message because they are derived from that very message. This also leads to consequent changes in beliefs and convictions and in the nature of relationships due to prophetic values displacing those of the pre-Islamic era.

The prophet's message attracted great attention in his society, similar to other prophets in their respective societies. His message addressed issues of interest to all people and shook that society to its core. This issue of relevance and influence sheds lights on the analysis we presented above regarding the impact of prophethood. Such impact extended beyond those who became faithful to the Prophet and his message; rather it extended to encompass all of society.

The values brought forth by the prophet led to changes in values and subsequently further led to deep and radical changes in relationships between individuals and groups as well as other social changes.

Grudges were buried because their underlying reasons no longer existed. The causes for outburst were extinguished, and thus those insurgencies were eradicated.

The entire society basked in a high degree of stability and peace after manifestations of violence and tension fell to the lowest levels as a result of the replacement of the prevailing concepts and values with the values propagated by prophethood.

These new values resulted in the establishment of new relationships.

God gave the prophet, through the values he preached to the people, brothers in the faith. These values in the faith separated the existing groups into new ones with different paths in response to the Prophet's message. Some groups followed the path of the faithful while the rest continued in their old ways set forth by the pre-Islamic era and its values.

These new values also led to changes in social classes. While the old values defined these classes based on money, pedigree, or military strength, the new values would replace these better values, such as piety.[12] God graced the Prophet with the values that overcame the humiliation of the poor and the weak, imposed by the old values of the pre-Islamic era, values that were rooted in things other than faith.

The Prophet's life is rife with hundreds of examples and illustrations from our Islamic history.

Oppressed individuals in pre-Islamic times, such as Ammar ibn Yasser and Bilal Al-Habashee, became venerated companions in the new society. That is because Islam nullified the values

---

[12] To understand the concept of Islamic piety, its components and implications, review our book "Studies in The Peak of Eloquence," Chapter on Society and Social Classes.

that forced them into humiliation and a low ranking social class. Islam brought forth new values that changed their social standing and made them among the elite. It also turned the tables on some of the elite of pre-Islamic times to lower social status. This is because they refused to improve themselves with the new values of piety and humility Islam brought forth. They persisted in their old ways and as such, humiliated themselves with their own backwardness.

* * *

The Imam discussed, in some of his texts in The Peak of Eloquence, the status of Arabs in light of the impact of prophethood on their moral and daily life.

In the following text, the Imam paints an image of the Arab society in pre-Islamic times on the eve of the Prophet's revelation. This image included all aspects of life including the spiritual, societal and ethical ones. He said:

> *Verily, God sent Muhammad (S) as a warner (against vice) for all the worlds and a trustee of His revelation, while you people of Arabia were following the worst religion and you resided among rough stones and venomous serpents. You drank dirty water and ate filthy food. You shed blood of each other and cared not for*

relationship. Idols are fixed among you and sins are clinging to you.[13]

They followed the worst religion.

The idols were among them and they directed their worship and supplications to those idols. As such, they were pagans and their paganism, borrowed from here and there, was primitive, void of artistic beauty and good taste in addition to its pre-ordained emptiness of proper spiritual content.

They resided in the worst places [among rough stones and venomous serpents]. They lived in arid lands under difficult and harsh conditions that subjected their lives to a series of threats, troubles and deprivation.

Because of the void in their spiritual lives and because of their difficult living conditions, they were in the worst shape in their social lives and human relationships. They spilt each other's blood and cut off their familial lines. They were constantly toiling just to provide for a hard backwards and poor life, poor in both form and content, in the shadows of corrupt social and human relations.

* * *

---

[13] The Peak of Eloquence, Sermon 26.

In another text, the Imam (a) provides insight into the changes brought forth by prophethood into the lives of Arabs. He details the general conditions before and after Islam. He said:

> *Certainly God Almighty sent Muhammad (S) as Prophet while no one among the Arabs read the Book nor claimed prophethood or revelation. He had to fight those who disobeyed him in company with those who followed him, leading them towards their salvation and hastening with them lest death overtook them. When any weary person sighed or a distressed one stopped he stood at him until he got him his aim, except the worst in whom there was not virtue at all. Eventually he showed them their goal and carried them to their places (of deliverance). Consequently, their affairs moved on and their hand-mill began to rotate (i.e. position gained strength), their spears got straightened.[14]*

Many Arabs were illiterate and ignorance was prevalent among them. They were far removed from prophethood and Divine messages and as such their spiritual lives were poor, miserable and distorted. The Prophet endeavored to bring them out of the darkness, all of the darkness: from the darkness of the soul, mind and life into all of the light; from backwardness into progress, from ignorance into knowledge, from spiritual blindness into the grace of the greater faith.

---

[14] The Peak of Eloquence, Sermon 104.

And thus he brought them to the shore of survival in this life and the hereafter. He gave them a universal role, as Muslims carrying guidance, enlightenment and dignity to all nations after they had been a insignificant group with no value or role. He offered them a better life with dignity and stability. Their lives were no longer harsh and difficult and their fortunes were reversed with bounty.

Their lives were no longer worrisome, obsessive and aggressive; rather they became settled and peaceful. Their world became less vulnerable, less inviting to aggressors and unoccupied by a constant need to respond to aggression. May God's peace and blessings be upon all the prophets and messengers.

AWARENESS OF HISTORY

It is certain that Arabs in the pre-Islamic times lacked historical consciousness, one that was characteristic of civilized peoples with recorded culture and established administrative and political institutions. This is in addition to a lack of historical consciousness as defined in the contemporary.

This is especially applicable to Arabs in the north even though Arabs in the south did not fare much better. The pre-Islamic Arabs lived a nomadic life with all of its necessary migration and movement in search of food and water. As such, Arabs did not have established institutions or political and administrative systems.

Illiteracy dominated this society and as result, a recorded culture of any kind did not develop, except for rare inscriptions that cannot amount to a chronicled culture or give us insight into these people's cultural identity. We are not excluding the Arabs in the south from this assessment. They lost many of their traits as a civilized society, one with a rich history, due to a collapse in their irrigation system. They consequently fell closer to nomadism and illiteracy.

Life was so simple and naïve that significant events within it were very rare and were also limited in scope geographically and people-wise. These events formed the so called "Arab Days" which we will discuss shortly.

Arabs in pre-Islamic times did not understand continuous time as a concept of civilization. Time for them was simply a succession of astronomical phenomena and season. It is also known that Arabs in pre-Islamic times did not have a system counting years.

As a result of all of the above factors, there are no historical events of significance for Arabs at that time, due to such events not actually occurring on the one hand and due to the people not realizing them as such on the other hand. There are only scattered unrelated events framed within the succession of time and internal relationships.

In other words, pre-Islamic Arabs did not have an awareness of the continuity of events, their everlasting impact, their internal relations, their connection to their own present, or their ability to impact their future in a manner that can be labeled awareness of history. Such a historical awareness was very limited among Arabs in pre-Islamic times. There was only a hint of such awareness among them.

Mysterious, foggy and distorted images of such a history emerged from genealogical records and from stories that were called "Ayyam [Days]." Such genealogy and stories make up the extent of the historical perspective of Arabs at that time. Certainly, such a hint of awareness of the past does not constitute a full consciousness of history as we define it today. For these stories did not cover the major events that impacted politics and humans of the time. That is what provides history its true meaning and essence. Most of the context of these stories consisted of small battles among tribal groups; these stories were subject to poetic imagination and texts that gave them unrealistic glory and scope. In addition, they did not have an element of interdependence nor did they take into account causality or internal relationships.

These stories were free from the element of time, not out of neglect; rather, it was caused by their ignorance of the impact of time on history as we mentioned above. These stories were passed at gatherings held in tents for the purpose of entertainment and passing time, and even for boasting in some cases. These exchanges were not scientific by any means and most likely the events were never recorded.

And while mentions of lineage indicated a sense of the past from the perspective of belonging to the ancestors, these were limited to just citing the names without the inclusion of any related historical context. In addition, these mentions were oral which nullifies their value in providing historical context. It is certain that family trees in pre-Islamic times were not recorded in any manner that allows adding a historical context to them. Recording of family trees did not start until a relatively later time in the Islamic era.

We get a brief insight into the pre-Islamic Arabs' sense of history through their attitude towards moral positions related to war, generosity, loyalty and the like. This is reflected through the people's worry about future stories reflecting behaviors that are not noble and so they modify their behaviors to be consistent with nobility values as defined by the morals of the pre-Islamic society: to be loyal, courageous until death and generous.

These feelings can be a preliminary basis of historical awareness however they do not amount to the level of historical awareness as we defined above. The latter is based on ingrained moral values and not limited to individual cases or to sentiments and feelings of a historical presence – feelings of apprehension from a personal behavior or position that may prompt condemnation from others versus a sense of achievement by others and interactions with those achievements.

* * *

Such was the state of the pre-Islamic Arabs. But the state of the Arabs changed completely with the advent of Islam.

The Holy Quran and the Tradition of the Prophet (s) gradually revealed to Arabs their impact on history as Muslims. Both sources slowly raised Muslims' awareness of their deep impact on history through stories of past nations, their prophets, their positions of said prophets, their state of prosperity, their decline and their destruction.

These stories helped Muslims realize, that through their religion, daily struggles (sword and word alike) within their own Muslim communities that are building themselves with God's help and under the Prophet's guidance, and in confronting the infidels, that they are building a history connected to that of previous nations as taught by the Book and the Tradition of the Prophet (s). As such came to be the historical awareness of the Muslim people.

* * *

History has a function beyond our sense of permanence; it is that of moral education. So even though we look to history for research and analysis, the ultimate goal from history is moral education.

This function derives its characteristics and form from the nature of the approach a nation follows in building itself and from the kind of the role it prepares itself to play regionally and globally. Therefore we see that every nation with unique intellectual characteristics makes history an integral building block for its chosen path.

However, this does not mean altering history so it is a propaganda and political tool. We must always respect our duty to the truth. It means that history is not a tool for mere entertainment or an intellectual pastime. History is a very dangerous matter when used by people with no morality, who are not motivated by a spiritual mission, or people and systems motivated by racial and national intolerance and arrogance. In these cases, history may be redirected to serve as theoretical justification and a psychological tool in the oppressive and aggressive tendencies of politics and war against other nations. In those cases, history is subject to misrepresentation and deception.

History is replete with examples where it is used for the purposes of unethical and missionary goals in ancient and in modern times. From this perspective, history in Islam has a function related to the nature of people and the nature of community in Islam. People in Islam are ones with morals and a universal message. Islamic society is one that is ethical espousing a comprehensive vision for humanity.

Therefore history must serve the moral and ethical aspects in the internal and external relationships of Muslims, just like it must serve the message and the spirit of the message in for the whole world.

Anytime the behavior of a Muslim person or group deviates from the morals or apostolic spirit in everyday life, history should be used, along with other educational and organizational means, to correct the erroneous perception and to straighten out the individual or group.

The Holy Quran is full of such examples, among them is an expression related to history. It is the "days of God" which means major events in the history of every nation, be it great successes and victories or great catastrophes and tragic crises.

The expression of "days of God" occurred only once in the Holy Quran. The expression was in the context of the verses where Prophet Moses (a) was guiding the children of Israel to the true faith and enhancing their level of knowledge from an ignorant, primitive and material state to one of faith and civilization. God Almighty said:

> *And certainly We sent Musa with Our communications, saying: Bring forth your people from utter darkness into light and remind them of the days of God; most surely there are signs in this for every patient, grateful one.*[1]

The same expression was mentioned twice in the Peak of Eloquence. The first is when the Imam was reciting God's words: "… there glorify Him therein in the mornings and the evenings, Men whom neither merchandise nor selling diverts from the remembrance of God…"[2] He said in describing them:

---

[1] The Holy Quran, 14:5.
[2] The Holy Quran, 24: 36-37.

... there have always been persons with whom God, precious are His bounties, whispered through their wits and spoke through their minds. With the help of the bright awakening of their ears, eyes and hearts they keep reminding others of the remembrance of the days of God and making others feel fear for Him....[3]

The second one is in a letter to his governor in Mecca, Qatham ibn al-Abbas.[4] He said: *"Now, make arrangements for Hajj by the people, remind them of the days of God..."*[5]

* * *

The Imam provided intellectual guidance, lectures, preaching and political direction from this perspective of history. He directed Muslims to be aware of history on that basis and to deal with it from the perspective that serves morals and the message.

Perhaps the Imam's lecture "al-Qasse'a"[6] is the best example of the Imam using history for the purpose of education, social

---

[3] The Peak of Eloquence, Sermon 222.

[4] Qatham ibn al-Abbas bin Abed al-Muttalib. He helped the Imam in preparing and burying Prophet Mohamad. He was the last one to exit the honorable grave. The Imam made him a representative in Mecca and he held that post until the martyrdom of the Imam. Kathem was martyred in Samarkand where he had gone with Saeed ibn Othman bin Affan during the time of Muawiya. His grave is famous in Samarkand and we had visited it while attending a religious conference in the area.

[5] The Peak of Eloquence, Letters and Sayings #67

[6] The Peak of Eloquence, Letter 29.

development, and awareness. We will study parts of this lecture shortly.

We can get a realistic idea of the Imam's efforts to increase the people's awareness of history when we notice that much of the Imam's words were focused on these related topics. Mind you what we have before us are only a small portion of all of his sayings and lectures. The Imam had addressed people at various times and situations, guiding their thinking through history with the objective of education and development in the spiritual, social and political matters of life. His focus was not reserved for preaching alone as it relates to these topics, as some may imagine.

Here are other examples related to the above in various quotes in The Peak of Eloquence:

> *You have been admonished through those who were before you....*
>
> *... So take admonishment, Oh servants of God, through effective patience....*
>
> *... And Beware of what had befallen the nations before you of disasters due to their evil deeds and reprehensible actions. Remember, in good times and bad, their tales. Beware, lest you become like them.*
>
> *... And take admonishment in [this world] from those who said, 'Who is more powerful than us?'*[7]

---

[7] The Holy Quran, 41:15.

There are many examples of such sayings in the Imam's lectures and letters. The Imam fought evil tendencies, delinquency and the strife that began sweeping through the Muslim society with every weapon; one of which was awareness of history.

HISTORY REPEATING ITSELF

Does history repeat itself?

It is obvious that history does not return to the present or the future if we meant the return of all of its details and events. Events are not isolated occurrences that happen in a vacuum with no connection to humanity. Rather events are made by humans and have the characteristics of their makers: they bear their specific interests, preferences, emotions, morals and their way of life. These characteristics disappear with their masters and never come back and in that exact sense, history does not return or repeat.

What happened in the past, happened one time only. What happened will not happen again. It will not repeat, ever.

If we meant the return of the same historical patterns, manifestations, and psychological and social impacts, then for sure, history does repeat itself. This would be when the original conditions that had led to its previous existence occur again in the present fiber of society and human relations.

Humans are humans at all times. Individuals, groups and entire communities are driven through time by their interests, relationships and emotions. Their beliefs, religion, ideals, and ethical and spiritual values are able to deeply impact their emotions, interests and relationships in their own society and world as a whole. This is particularly when they are deeply rooted in their conscience and are conditioning their view of the universe, life and other humans.

History will repeat itself when beliefs, religion, ideals, and ethical and spiritual values are not deeply rooted in a person. It is when people fail at prompting the appropriate change on the psychological human composition, along with the inability to assess their own interests and at impacting their perception of the world, life and humanity.

In all likelihood, this new history will not exhibit the same traits and characteristics as it did in the past. However it will carry the same spirits and it will leave similar impacts on society as the past had. This of course would be under new names and with new justifications that are no more than misleading superficial veneer. Historians are able to uncover what is behind that veneer and delve deep to discover the same reality brought in a new form.[1]

* * *

In his first sermon after he was paid allegiance as Caliph in Medina, Imam Ali (a) noticed the return of the old ways of tribal divisions and factions. They came with all of their tribal spirit, prejudices, and backwards values from the pre-Islamic Arab world. This occurred to the Muslim community during the reign of Othman and subsequently after his death.

The return of these old values, with their backwards content, was a result of atrophy in the high ideals and effective values of Islam. It was also the result of weaknesses in the institution of the Caliphate during the time of Othman. This weakness allowed the old forces and ideals, which had not yet died but rather were in a state of subsidence and atrophy, to regain their effectiveness and once again impact history through slogans that were only exteriorly compatible with Islam.

These old values and ideals of pre-Islamic times drove the impact of history in Arab society, defined its characteristics and guided its path prior to the emergence of Prophet Muhammad

---

[1] We believe that the phenomenon of regional divisions in the Arab world is among the important ones worthy of in-depth research by historians and thinkers. We believe such a division is a new expression of tribalism, under new names and with justifications that are suitable for the current cultural climate and prevailing political awareness. We believe that the failure of the idea of Arab unity is not solely due to sabotage by colonialism but it grew out of a readiness for fragmentation. This readiness helped colonialism to shape its policies and their success and helped it attain its goals.

and the triumph of Islam. These values were reemerging and becoming effective once again.

The Commander of the Faithful Ali saw these old and reemerging values by monitoring new phenomena that appeared among groups in the Muslim community its leaders that were guiding such groups, openly and secretly.

He also saw the impacts that this backwards and evil movement would once again have on history in Islam and the catastrophes that would befall Muslims as individuals, groups, society, nation and institutions.

He said:

> *The responsibility for what I say is guaranteed and I am answerable for it. He to whom experiences have clearly shown the past exemplary punishments (given by God to peoples) is prevented by piety from falling into doubts. You should know that the same troubles have returned to you which existed when the Prophet was first sent.*
>
> *By God who sent the Prophet with faith and truth, you will be severely subverted, bitterly shaken as in sieving and fully mixed as by spooning in a cooking pot until your low persons become high and high ones become low, those who were behind would attain forward positions and those who were forward would become backward...*[2]

---

[2] The Peak of Eloquence, Sermon 16.

He told them of the return of the "troubles" (social corruption and moral and cultural decadence) that were characteristic of Arab life in the pre-Islamic era. This return would be due to the rising prevalence of the values of that time and the perspective of those times towards the universe, life and humanity. These troubles had returned to the same level as they had been on the eve of the Prophet receiving his message. These values had renewed and that came at the expense of the new values of Islam, whose influence had been reduced due to various factors. This led to gaps in the new values through which the old values found renewed life.

Imam Ali warned his community that these reemerging troubles will have tragic consequences for Muslim society. These troubles will lead to social crises and revolts that will throw society into the clutches of a destructive civil war and no doubt, these crises and wars will be worse and more deadly than the ones during pre-Islamic times. The community will also experience mayhem as a result of these crises and revolts which will in turn generate more chaos. The community will become like a boiling pot where ingredients are all mixed and which does not settle on a certain path or enjoy peace. Instead the community is in a constant state of turmoil and unrest.

This will lead to the separation of the different groups and the definition of their characteristics, just like trials and tribulations usually do. However, all that will occur will not include any good but will result in evil for society. It will disrupt the community in a manner that paralyzes effectiveness, disrupts or even threatens positive impacts, and impedes the movement of progress.

This will be the return of the pre-Islamic times under the guise of Islam sent forth by the values of those times, which have come back to life. They will become the underlying reasons for the movement of Muslims in time and place instead of the new Islamic values.

Such was the depiction of history repeating itself by the Imam.

* * *

After Zubair ibn Awam, Talha ibn Khuwaylid and Aisha turned against the Imam (a), the doors to civil strife and civil war were opened. It engulfed the Muslims in turmoil and tore apart their unity as predicted by the Imam (a). Subsequently, on his way from the city of Basra he gave a sermon at Dhi Qar.[3] He likened his march to confront the first signs of disorder to his march with the Prophet to confront the forces of pre-Islamic times. He also stated that the motivation behind each march was the same, despite their external differences. It may have meant one thing to the naïve, but it was surely understood by experts.

---

[3] Dhi Qar: An area near Basra that is best known in history as the place where the first signs of Islam appeared. In 610 AD, 3,000 Arabs from the tribe of Bakr bin Wael attacked this area in the Euphrates and they decisively defeated the Persians in Dhi Qar.

The Imam (a) said:

> By God, surely I was in their lead until it took shape with
> its walls. I did not show weakness or cowardice. My
> existing march is also like that. I shall certainly pierce the
> wrong until right comes out of its side. What (cause of
> conflict) is there between me and the Quraysh? By God, I
> have fought them when they were unbelievers and I shall
> fight them when they have been misled. I shall be the
> same for them today as I was for them yesterday...[4]

The Imam was talking about the role of pre-Islamic times in
confronting Islam and about his struggle with the Messenger
of God against pre-Islamic times. He then likened his march to
Basra as no different than the signs of stubbornness that he and
the Prophet confronted from pre-Islamic times.

History had repeated itself, but under a different guise.

Ibn Hadid said in explaining this text:

> He likened the matter of pre-Islamic times to rebelling or
> to battalion approaching war. He said, 'I banished it and
> it ran from my grasp. I stayed on its trail. I banish it and
> it runs from me until it left in its entirety and there was
> nothing left of it. I did not fail in this nor was I coward
> in facing it.' He then said, 'My existing march is also like
> that. I shall certainly pierce the wrong...' It was as if he

---

[4] The Peak of Eloquence, Sermon 33.

made the wrong something that had engulfed and overtaken the right. It contained the right which became hidden within it. He vowed to pierce that wrong until the right could come out of it.[5]

Thus the Imam depicted history repeating itself, when the old reasons that resulted in the old events and situations are functioning again. They led to the repetition of situations and events but under new banners commensurate with the prevailing culture in the community.

There are other texts, besides the ones we mentioned, throughout the Peak of Eloquence showcasing this truth.

---

[5] Ibn Abi Hadid – Shareh Nahj Al-Balagha by Mohamad Abu al-Fadl Ibrahim. Dar Ehya' al-Koutob al-Arabeyah – Cairo. First edition. 1378 AH – 1959 AD. Volume 2. Pages 185-186.

LESSONS FROM THE CENTURIES

Imam Ali (a) used the expression "lessons from the Centuries" in one of his sermons, saying "take a lesson from what you have seen about the falling places of those before you."[1] The Imam (a) meant past generations and previous centuries by this expression; centuries in Arabic was used to indicate a group of people in the same era.[2] In this expression, the Imam is guiding the thought process towards contemplation of the destinies of nations and peoples; how and why they became weak, failed, degenerated or went backwards.

---

[1] The Peak of Eloquence, Sermon 161.

[2] This word was used extensively in the Holy Quran in chapters from Medina and from Mecca. It would seem that it was intended to mean a measure of time. It was said: a century is the age for most people, around seventy years. Some said around eighty years and some said thirty years. It was also said: A century is a measure of a period of time that has its own prophet or scholar; it was used in the context of 'his time or more.' This last meaning signifies a cultural sense for the word.

The Imam (a) asks in another sermon, potentially his last one to a large group,[3] about the fate of olden nations and peoples, saying to his companions:

> ... *Certainly, the by-gone centuries have a lesson for you. Where are the Amalekites [giants] and the sons of Amalekites? Where are the Pharaohs? Where are the people of the cities of ar-Rass who killed the prophets, destroyed the traditions of the divine messengers and revived the traditions of the despots? Where are those who advanced with armies, defeated thousands, mobilized forces and populated cities?*[4]

* * *

The internal conditions of society during the Imam Ali's (a) rule compelled him to utilize history to face what was deteriorating in that society. Especially in Iraq, society suffered from tribal divisions, prejudiced attitudes, oppression by the

---

[3] Al-Sharif said in the Peak of Eloquence: "It has been related by Nawf al-Bikali that the Commander of the Faithful `Ali (a) delivered this sermon at Kufah standing on a stone which Ja`dah ibn Hubayrah al-Makhzumi had placed for him. The Commander of the Faithful had a woolen apparel on his body, the belt of his sword was made of leaves, and the sandals on his feet too were of palm leaves. His forehead had a hardened spot like that a camel (on its knee, due to many and long prostrations). He said, 'Then the Commander of the Faithful put Husayn (a) over (a force of) ten thousand, Qays ibn Sa`d (mercy of God be upon him) over ten thousand, Abu Ayyub al-Ansari over ten thousand, and others over different numbers, intending to return to Siffin, but Friday did not appear again and the accursed Ibn Muljam (may God curse him) killed him. Consequently, the armies came back and were left like sheep who had lost their shepherd while wolves were snatching them away from all sides.'" [Source: the Peak of Eloquence, Sermon 182]

[4] The Peak of Eloquence, sermon 182.

heads of tribes against their own tribes, and the fascination of many of the thinkers and leaders in society with the excesses about which they had heard Muawiyah bestowed upon his political supporters. The Imam (a) knew from his sharp foresight that this approach would lead society towards ruin. Internal conflict will exhaust it, weaken its infrastructure, do away with its unity, drive its leaders to betraying their communities and throwing themselves at the oppressive regime of the Umayyads in Syria. It would lead Iraq to lose its leadership role in the caliphate, rendering it as inferior to the position of Syria.

Imam Ali faced this danger with various approaches and at different levels. One of the approaches he used at the grassroots level was reflection on history as it relates to the state of the community. He strived to ensure that regular people had an awareness of history and a realistic vision of the present to help them realize and sense the dangers from the practices prevalent in society. He intended all this so he instills in their hearts and minds caution and foresight when they are faced with choices that had causes previous nations catastrophes that weakened or destroyed them.

It is important to note that when the Imam (a) talks of the degeneration of nations and the lessons from the previous centuries, he is not providing theoretical reasons but rather he is presenting objective reasons for this decadence, as we will see later.

The best example from the Peak of Eloquence about this topic is the sermon called "al-Qasse'a".[5] In this sermon, the Imam described the breakdowns that subjected the Iraqi society to danger. He recounted the related historical perspectives and the reasons for that decadence.

* * *

The sermon addressed a very dangerous and growing issue that was festering in the Iraqi community at that time. That was the issue of internal conflict which was ripping the Iraqi community apart, paralyzing its effectiveness and reflecting badly on the rest of the nations in the caliphate.

To an observer, this conflict seemed to have many facets:

TRIBAL CONFLICT

The tribal spirit and values had reappeared and become active, imposing their logic on the social and political relations within society. The reemergence of the tribal spirit was a result to a host of mistakes committed during the time of the third

---

[5] Ibn Hadid said in explaining this word: "It is acceptable to name this sermon 'al-Qasse'a' from their saying, 'The camel took down its jug, meaning it either swallowed or spit it in order to fill its mouth. Admonishments and lessons from this sermon were repeated just like a camel that takes its jug in and out of its mouth. It is possible that it was called al-Qasse'a because it kills Satan and his followers, similar to the saying 'it killed the ant for it disfigured it and killed it.' It is possible that it was called al-Qasse'a in order to inspire less arrogance and pride in the audience, just like the saying 'the water did away with his thirst, or it made it go away.'" Source: Shareh Nahj Al-Balagha, volume 13, page 128.

caliphate, Othman ibn Affan. These mistakes spanned the political, administrative, economical and general cultural facets.

It would seem that this tribal spirit caused widespread damage in the Iraqi society. We believe that Muawiya ibn Abi Sufyan further exploited this discord to cause further rifts in the unity of Iraqi society.

It would also seem that tribal spirit, which was fueled by special interests, succeeded to a large extent in disrupting the unity of Iraq, fueling suspicion and hatred among and within the political classes. This is conveyed to us in one of the Imam's (a). Warning and reprimanding his community, he said:

> *...You are joined together in hatred of each other and in the growing of herbage on your filth (i.e., for covering inner dirt by good appearance outside). You are sincere with one another in your love of desires and bear enmity against each other in earning wealth. The evil spirit (Satan) has perplexed you and deceit has misled you. I seek the help of God for myself and you.*[6]

Ibn Abi al-Hadid described, in his explanation of the Peak of Eloquence, the sabotage and disruption caused by this tribal spirit. He said,

> *It is said that the origin of this prejudice and this sermon was that the people of Kufa had become corrupt towards*

---

[6] The Peak of Eloquence, Sermon 133.

the latter part of the caliphate of the Commander of the Faithful. Kufa had multiple tribes and a young man would leave the area of his own tribe and walk around the homes of another tribe calling out the name of his own tribe. For example, he would say, 'O Nkha!' or 'O Kindah!' intending to provoke discord and malignity. This caused the young men from the other tribes to call out, 'O Tameem!' or 'O Rabee'ah!' and then they would come to that person and beat him up. He would then go back to his own tribe, asking for their help. And so swords would be unsheathed and tempers would rise. And there was no basis for this discord other than young men bickering with each other.[7]

However, where Ibn Abi Hadid did not see an underlying point of origin, we see the hand of Muawiya and his agents. They encouraged such tribal practices and fueled it with more reasons for excitement and unrest in order to further tire and rupture Iraqi society. We also see the politics of the tribal leaders behind this discord, for Imam Ali's (a) policies threatened their power and influence. Thus, they encouraged the public and the simple-minded to commit such behaviors so they could reassert their influence with their own tribes.

---

[7] Ibn Abi Hadid, Shareh Nahj Al-Balagha, volume 13, pages 167-168.

RACIAL CONFLICT

Like other Muslim nations at the time, the Iraqi community included large groups of non-Arab Muslims. Many of them had converted to Islam after conquests beyond the Arabian Peninsula. Those conquests led to the occupation of their own countries in Iran and the Byzantine Empire (Egypt, Syria and others).

In theory, these people had equal rights and equal responsibilities to Arab Muslims. Islam had guaranteed them the exact same rights as Arab Muslims. However, in reality, they suffered from racial discrimination because of the tribal spirit and Arab prejudice.

After coming into power, Imam Ali (a) immediately put an end to all forms of racial discrimination and prejudice from which non-Arab Muslims suffered.

This drew negative feedback from the tribal leaders. They objected to the equality in bestowments between them and the non-Arab Muslims, saying,

> *O Commander of the Faithful, give these monies and favor the nobles of Arabs and Quraish over the non-Muslim Arabs and the foreigners. Gain the favor of those who you fear causing discord among the people.*[8]

---

[8] Ibn Abi Hadid, Shareh Nahj Al-Balagha.

The source of this advice and the political perspective of these leaders were from Muawiya's directives.

However, Imam Ali (a) persisted in his political practices from another perspective, saying to them,

> *Do you command me that I should seek support by oppressing those over whom I have been placed? By God, I won't do so as long as the world goes on, and as long as one star leads another in the sky...*[9]

The al-Qasse'a sermon includes many other indications that the racial conflict and not just the ingrained tribal one by itself, was behind Imam Ali's (a) deep concerns.

This conflict, both tribal and racial, was a bane in itself and it generated other banes.

1. It deepened and strengthened the tribal social reality, as well as the tribal structure of society in the general culture and the individual psychological makeup. It thus prevented the evolution of the social structure from lineage-based tribal mentality to a unified system based on belief, law, institutions and common interests. This also led to a social paralysis that held society in a state of backwardness as it relates to institutions and organizational achievements.

---

[9] The Peak of Eloquence, Sermon 126.

2. It increased and strengthened the authority of the tribal chiefs over their people and that weakened the effectiveness of the central governing bodies.

3. It impacted the cohesion of society, which was in a state of war with external forces in Syria and the Kharijites.

4. Through the tribes, it strengthened the ability of Muawiyah to infiltrate the political institutions in Iraqi society.

* * *

We now turn to the evidence in the al-Qasse'a sermon. The Imam revealed that pride is one of God's attributes and as such, it is not for people to show pride over one other.

He then reminded the people of Satan and his pride and prejudice against Adam, boasting of his own origin. He reminded them that Satan's pride was his undoing and how it destroyed his high stature.

The Imam (a) then compared Satan's pride to that of human and he considered the proud ones to be followers of Satan because of this reprehensible attribute:

> ... yet the sons of vanity, the brothers of haughtiness and the horsemen of pride and intolerance proved him to be true, so much so that when disobedient persons from among you bowed before him, and his greed about you gained strength; and what was a hidden secret turned

into a clear fact, he spread his full control over you... In this way he became more harmful to your religion and a greater kindler of flames (of mischief) about your worldly matters than the enemies against whom you showed open opposition and against whom you marched your forces.[10]

And thus the Imam (a) showed them that the evil and corruption that are borne out of prejudice, as well as the resulting struggles, do not just affect the religion and the faith but also impact the realities of religious life. The people were being prejudiced against those they feared would impact their material advantages.

The Imam then reminded them of the story of the son of Adam, a familiar historical event from the Quran:

... Do not be like him who feigned superiority over the son of his own mother without any distinction given to him by God except the feeling of envy which his feeling of greatness created in him and the fire of anger that vanity kindled in his heart. Satan blew into his nose his own vanity, after which God gave him remorse and made him responsible for the sins of all killers up to the Day of Judgement.[11]

---

[10] The Peak of Eloquence, Sermon 192, also known as al-Qasse'a.
[11] The Peak of Eloquence, Sermon 192.

Once again, the Imam (a) reprimands his audience for their tribal spirit and despised racial intolerance, indicating to them that this dangerous bane had plagued previous nations and made them taste its bitterness:

Beware! You strove hard in revolting and created mischief on the earth in open opposition to God and in challenging the believers over fighting. (You should fear) God! God! in feeling proud of your vanity and boasting over ignorance, because this is the root of enmity and the design of Satan wherewith he has been deceiving past people and bygone ages... In this matter the hearts of all the people were similar, and centuries passed by, one after the other, in just the same way, and there was vanity with which chests were tightened.[12]

He then directly drew attention to the leadership that encourages this misery and fans its flames, the leaders of the tribes:

Beware! Beware of obeying your leaders and elders who felt proud of their achievements and boasted about their lineage... Certainly, they are the main foundation of obstinacy, the chief pillars of mischief and the swords of pre-Islamic boasting over forefathers. Therefore, fear God, do not become antagonistic to His favours on you,

---

[12] The Peak of Eloquence, Sermon 192.

nor jealous of His bounty over you and do not obey the claimants (of Islam) whose dirty water you drink along with your clean one, whose ailments you mix with your healthiness and whose wrongs you allow to enter into your rightful matters. They are the foundation of vice and the linings of disobedience...[13]

The Imam (a) then refers to history, reiterating the tragic fate of nations and people who were affected by the bane of intolerance and rivalry, comparing that to the prophetic path for human that is far removed from pride:

Take instruction from how God's wrath, violence, chastisement and punishment fell upon the arrogant nations before you. Take admonition from the resting places of their cheeks and their bodies... Certainly, if God were to allow anyone to indulge in pride He would have allowed it to his selected prophets and vicegerents... When Musa son of `Imran went to Pharaoh along with his brother Harun (Aaron) wearing (coarse) shirts of wool and holding sticks in their hands, they guaranteed him retention of his country and continuity of his honour if he submitted; but he said: "Do you not wonder at these two men guaranteeing me the continuity of my honour

---

[13] The Peak of Eloquence, Sermon 192.

and the retention of my country although you see their poverty and lowliness.[14]

The Imam (a) continues in his glance at history, calling on his listeners to examine the historical situations that previous nations experienced. In that reflection he was asking them to avoid the trials and tribulations that led to decadence and collapse of these nations. He asked them to choose the paths that have been proven worthy through experience.

You should also fear what calamities befell peoples before you on account of their evil deeds and detestable actions. Remember, during good or bad circumstances, what happened to them, and be cautious that you do not become like them. After you have thought over both the conditions of these people, attach yourself to everything with which their position became honorable, on account of which enemies remained away from them through which safety spread over them, by reason of which riches bowed before them and as a result of which distinction connected itself with their rope. These things were abstention from division, sticking to unity, calling each other to it and advising each other about it. You avoid everything which broke their backbone and weakened their power, such as malice in the heart, hatred in the chest, turning away

---

[14] The Peak of Eloquence, Sermon 192.

(from each other's help) and withholding the hand from one another's assistance.[15]

The Imam (a) continues in his historical look and provides specific examples from the lives of Arabs and Israelites, after his general reflection on nations that passed:

Think about the condition of people from among the believers who passed before you. What distresses and trials they were in! Were they not the most over-burdened among all the people and in the most straitened circumstances in the whole world? The Pharaohs took them as slaves. They inflicted on them the worst punishments and bitter sufferings. They continuously remained in this state of ruinous disgrace and severe subjugation... Until when God, the Glorified, noticed that they were enduring troubles in His love and bearing distresses out of fear for Him, He provided escape from the distress of trials. So, He changed their disgrace into honor and fear into safety. Consequently, they became ruling kings and conspicuous leaders...

Look, how they were when their groups were united, their views were unanimous, their hearts were moderate, their hands used to help one another, their swords were intended for assisting one another, their eyes were sharp and their aims were the same. Did they not become

---

[15] The Peak of Eloquence, Sermon 192.

masters of the corners of the earth and rulers over the neck of all the worlds?

Thereafter, also see what happened to them towards the end when division overtook them, unity became fractured, and differences arose between their words and their hearts. They divided into various groups and were scattered fighting among themselves. Then God took away from them the apparel of His honor and deprived them of the prosperity produced by His favors. Only their stories have remained among you for the guidance of those who may learn the lesson from them.

You should take a lesson from the fate of the progeny of Ismael, the children of Isaac and the children of Israel. How similar are their affairs and how akin are their examples. In connection with the details of their division and disunity, think of the days when Kisras of Persia and the Caesars of Rome had become their masters. They turned them out from the pastures of their lands, the rivers of Iraq and the fertility of the world, towards thorny forests, the passages of (hot) winds and hardships in livelihood. In this way they turned them into just herders of camels. Their houses were the worst in the world and their places of stay were the most drought-stricken. There was not one voice towards which they could turn for protection, nor any shade of affection on whose strength they could repose trust. Their condition was full of distress. Their hands were scattered. Their majority was divided. They were in great anguish and under layers of ignorance. They buried their daughters alive, worshipped idols, disregarded kinship and practised robbery.

Now, look at the various favours of God upon them, that He deputed towards them a prophet who got them to pledge their obedience to him and made them unite at his call. (Look) how (God's) bounty spread the wings of its favours over them and flowed for them streams of its blessing, and the whole community became wrapped in blissful prosperity. Consequently, they were submerged under its bounty and enjoyed its lush life. Their affairs were settled under the protection of a powerful ruler, and circumstances offered them overpowering honor, and all things became easy for them under the auspices of a strong country. They became rulers over the world and kings in the (various) parts of the earth. They became masters of those who were formerly their masters, and began issuing commands over those who used to command them. They were so strong that neither did their spears need testing nor did their weapons have any flaw.

Certainly, there are examples before you of God's wrath, punishment, days of tribulations and happenings. Therefore, do not disregard His promises, ignoring His punishment, making light His wrath and not expecting

His violence, because God, the Glorified, did not curse the past ages except because they had left off asking others to do good acts and refraining them from bad acts. In fact God cursed the foolish for committing sins and the wise because they gave up refraining others from evils...[16]

---

[16] The Peak of Eloquence, Sermon 192.

GOOD, EVIL, AND THE
SILENT MAJORITY

One of the greatest tenets of Islam is the enjoining of good and forbidding of evil. The sanctioning of this duty was mentioned in several texts in the Holy Book and in the honorable Sunnah, signifying the necessity of enjoining good and forbidding evil for all Muslims as a collective duty.[1]

Many of those texts include details on the conditions requiring this obligation on Muslims. Some of these texts shed light on

---

[1] Religious jurists divide duties into categories, among which are *'Ayni* [duties that must be upheld by Muslims on an individual level] and *Kifaei* [collective duties that must be upheld by society as a whole]. Concrete duties are the ones required of each obligated person [of age] and this duty remains even if someone else is fulfilling. A collective duty is one that requires the presence of the action regardless of which obligated person performs it; it is a duty of all obligated persons but it is sufficient when some of them perform it, making it no longer required of the rest of them. If all obligated persons neglected the collective duty, then they have all sinned. Examples of collective duties are abundant and include preparing the dead and praying for them. They also include vocations, industries and occupations upon which the structure of life for the people is dependent, including jurisprudence in the religious laws and enjoining good and forbidding evil.

the political and social aspects of this obligation. They also clarify the general Muslim intellectual principle from which this obligation emerges. This obligation is stated in the Holy Book when God says,

> *And from among you there should be a party who invite*
> *to good and enjoin what is right and forbid the wrong,*
> *and these it is that shall be successful.*[2]

This verse demonstrates the obligation of enjoining good and forbidding evil with the use of the word "should" signaling obligation.

This verse seems to indicate that this obligation is collective and not concrete, because the intended consequence is to have among the Muslims a group who gives orders and prohibits. It is not intended that each of them does so and if some of them fulfill this obligation, then the obligation is no longer required from the rest of them, as would have been true of concrete obligations.

The number of people fulfilling this obligation is not specified in the Holy Quran or in the Sunnah and that is so the number of people fulfilling this obligation is commensurate with the need for it.

---

[2] The Holy Quran, 3:104.

God Almighty provided awareness of this obligation and the need to fulfill it when He included among the qualities of the righteous believers the performance of this obligation,

> *And (as for) the believing men and the believing women,*
> *they are guardians of each other; they enjoin good and*
> *forbid evil and keep up prayer and pay the poor-rate, and*
> *obey God and His Apostle; (as for) these, God will show*
> *mercy to them; surely God is Mighty, Wise.*[3]

This blessed verse shows the collaboration of the believers in the area of good deeds, righteousness and piety and that they are soldiers to this obligation when duty calls for it.

The context of the verse indicates the obligation of enjoining good and forbidding evil in that the remainder of the verse states the known obligations in the religion (prayer, tithing, and obeying God and His Messenger)[4] However contextual indications are not necessary to prove religious legal provisions.

Just like the aforementioned verse praises the believing men and women, as individuals, so does another verse bring praise to Muslims in general, as a nation and a society, in regards to their awareness and fulfillment of this obligation. God said,

---

[3] The Holy Quran, 9:71.

[4] It is possible that the intended meaning of obeying God and His Messenger is in the political sense because the mention of the specific (enjoining good and forbidding evil, prayers, and tithing) is done before the mention of the general.

You are the best of the nations raised up for (the benefit of) men; you enjoin what is right and forbid the wrong and believe in God... [5]

In His Holy Book, God praised the people of the Book, the followers of previous prophets before the start of Prophet Muhammad's message, for their awareness and fulfillment of this duty. This points to the agedness of this as a duty in Islam since its most ancient eras and that it was a fixed duty in all of the religion's legislative stages brought on by God's prophets, generation after generation. God says,

They are not all alike; of the followers of the Book there is an upright party; they recite God's communications in the nighttime and they adore (Him). They believe in God and the last day, and they enjoin what is right and forbid the wrong and they strive with one another in hastening to good deeds, and those are among the good. [6]

* * *

Reviving this duty and making it one of the concerns of society was a continuous issue for the Imam (a). He addressed it in his sermons and his speeches as we see from the examples provided to us in the Peak of Eloquence from various angles:

---

[5] The Holy Quran, 3:110.
[6] The Holy Quran, 3: 113-114.

The Imam (a) addressed this as an intellectual issue that had to be raised in order to enrich the conscious individuals and because it is a legislative issue inviting the nation and the individuals to work. From these two perspectives, he addressed it in a number of ways.

* * *

He gave it a great status, undoubtedly deserved, among the other religious duties and as such he made it one of the four branches of struggling:

> *Jihad also has four aspects: to ask others to do good, to keep away others from doing evil, to fight (in the way of God) sincerely and firmly on all occasions, and to detest the vicious. So, whoever asks others to do good provides strength to the believers; whoever desists others from evil humiliates the unbelievers; whoever fights sincerely on all occasions discharges all his obligations; and whoever detests the vicious and becomes angry for the sake of God, then God will be angry in favour of him and will keep him and will keep him pleased on the Day of Judgement.*[7]

The Imam put this obligation ahead of all good deeds in other speeches, saying:

---

[7] The Peak of Eloquence, Selections and Speeches, Hadith number 31.

...All the virtuous deeds including war in the way of God as compared to the persuasion to good and dissuasion from evil are just like spitting in the deep ocean...[8]

It is easy for us to understand advancing this obligation ahead of others if we noted that good deeds come after establishing an upright society with good principles, both legal and moral. We should also note that struggling is not effective unless done by a group of believers. All of this is a result of community awareness of and conformance to laws and ethics.

The Imam showcased part of the rationale for this law in some of his speeches, saying:

God has obligated... [that] persuasion for good for the good of the common people; dissuasion from evil for the control of the mischievous...[9]

For people who commit the sin of neglecting their duties because they do not fully know them or they are unaware of them, enjoining good educates them of their religious duties. In addition, it returns those that are derelict in their duties back to the righteous path. This is even when they are aware of those duties, and it puts on the good path the lost ones who transgress God's limits in their fun and play.

* * *

---

[8] The Peak of Eloquence, Selections and Speeches, Hadith number 374.

[9] The Peak of Eloquence, Selections and Speeches, Hadith number 252.

Enjoining good and forbidding evil has many levels. It is a flexible obligation that adapts to the need of varied situations and cases. Some people benefit from a simple word while others are only affected through force.

Each case has its own needs that would be assessed by the person enjoining the good and forbidding the evil. He should act only as needed, without exceeding the need or falling short of it. This is so the act itself does not negatively impact the ability of deterring the wrongdoer from his behavior and helping him to the righteous and straight path.

There are some cases of enjoining good and forbidding evil that require fighting. These cases require the leadership of a just ruler. In these very dangerous situations, it is not permissible for individuals or their communities to act without the leadership of a just and legitimate ruler.

If the levels of enjoining good and forbidding evil progress from condemning in the heart to condemning by the tongue to condemning by the hand, each with its own levels... And if the normal situations for enjoining good and forbidding evil vary in severity and importance which necessitates this level or other of condemnation... Then the severe cases that require the intervention of a just ruler and the whole nation could reach a degree of risk where condemnation by the heart, tongue and, in the most severe cases, the hand – meaning force – are necessary.

This is what the Muslim society was facing during the time of Imam Ali (a). At times, it was the transgressors who went back on their allegiance, stepped outside of the religious laws and attacked the city of Basra. The Imam's (a) message calling on them to return to his obedience went unheeded and they forced him to enter into the battle of the "Jamel" [Camel] against them in Basra. Rebels against the rule of law and the religion, under the leadership of Muawiya ibn Abi Sufyan in Syria, came forth to wage another civil war – Siffin. Their leader, Muawiya, refused all forms of policies that the Imam (a) proposed to him and would not return to the bounds of the religion. It was later the rogue Kharijites who would also refused all offers of peace and insisted on sedition and terrorism against farmers and innocent women and children.

In such cases, it is obligatory on the upright Muslim to renounce transgression by heart, condemn it publicly with his tongue and to engage in organized efforts led by the just ruler to straighten this transgression by force, when necessary.

In an apparent clarification for his followers from the dangerous deviation of principle, which was threatening the stability, progress, and unity of the entire Muslim society, the Imam (a) said:

> *So, among them (the Muslim community) there is he who disapproves evil with his hand, tongue and heart. This man has perfectly attained the virtuous habits. And*

among them there is he who disapproves evil with his tongue and heart but not with his hand. This man has attained only two virtuous habits but lacks one. And among them there is the third one who disapproves evil with his heart but not with his tongue and hand. This is the one who lacks the two better qualities out of three and holds only one. Then, among them there is also he who does not disapprove evil either with his tongue, heart or hand. He is just a dead man among the living.[10]

Here we note that, in the grave situations, the Imam (a) called he who abandons the duty of enjoining good and forbidding evil the "dead man among the living." The implication of this description is that a man who does not sense the dangers threatening his community and does nothing about it (even the condemnation in the heart which would require isolating and cutting off the transgressors) is like a dead body. The dead body does not reacts to any stimulus because such a body is void of life that feels and responds.

Abdul Rahman ibn Abi Layla al-Faqih was among those who fought alongside the Imam (a) in Siffin. He relates that Imam Ali (a) told them when they met the people of Syria:

O believers, whoever observes excesses being committed and people being called towards evil and disapproves it

---

[10] The Peak of Eloquence, Selections and Speeches, Hadith number 374.

with his heart is safe and free from responsibility for it, and whoever disapproves of it with his tongue would be rewarded and he is in a higher position than the former but whoever disapproves it with his sword in order that the word of God may remain superior and the word of the oppressors may remain inferior, catches hold of the path of guidance and stands on the right way, while his heart is lighted with conviction.[11]

Here we note that the Imam (a) put a condition on the highest form of forbidding evil – the form of using the sword. This condition is that the purpose of using the sword must be to uphold the word of God and not to serve familial prejudice, racism, personal interests or personal passions. This is a requirement for all human acts and at all levels of enjoining good and forbidding evil. The Imam (a) verbalized this need because of the seriousness of the implications of this level of condemnation since it could lead to wounding or killing others.

* * *

Imam Ali (a) estimated that many people fall short in exercising this great duty. They did not enjoin good to those who abandoned it nor did they forbid evil from those who committed it. Their inaction is due to perceived potential damage to them from doing so: exposing their lives to danger,

---

[11] The Peak of Eloquence, Selections and Speeches, Hadith number 373.

risking their social relationships, or endangering their livelihoods or other such concerns.

Such worries were noted by the religious legislator. Thus, the obligation of enjoining good and forbidding evil is conditioned on the lack of any significant harm that would be foreseeably inflicted on the individual carrying out this obligation.

However, many people do not want to be affected by any harm. Such an interested is a personal and self-centered one, one that should not be accepted by a person who is supposedly bound by the issues in his community like enjoining good and forbidding evil. Such a person is overcome by concern from any transgression he witnesses. His concern and morals push him to stand against any deviation in the proper manner. That is the person whom the Imam (a) meant in the above text when he talked about the "man [who] has perfectly attained the virtuous habits."

The Imam (a) warned through two separate topics in the Peak of Eloquence that failing to enjoin good and forbid evil out of fear of harm is based in illusions. A believer who is committed to his community should be able to overcome such illusions. A believer should not obsess over that fear, letting it paralyze him and get in between himself and blessed fruitful action. When the people of Basra were in need of direction because of the hardships witnessed in their city and because of the involvement of many in temptation, the Imam (a) said:

Commanding for good and refraining from evil are two attributes of God, the Glorified. They can neither bring death near nor lessen sustenance.[12]

Here we draw further attention to the Imam's (a) words. He says that enjoining good and forbidding evil are two characteristics from God Almighty, for God is the Commander of all that is good and the Forbidder of all that is evil. Therefore, a pious believer who is committed to his community and aware of the potential dangers surrounding it is in fact complying with God when he enjoins in good.

On another occasion, the Imam (a) said:

The persuasion for good and dissuasion from evil do not bring death nearer nor do they lessen livelihood.[13]

* * *

As we had said, the Imam (a) was constantly preoccupied with reviving the duty of enjoining good and forbidding evil. He wanted it to constantly capture the attention of the community and to make it a dynamic intellectual movement in that society.

There were two factors motivating his actions.

* First, he was the Imam (leader) of the Muslims and the Commander of the Faithful. Among his greatest duties

---

[12] The Peak of Eloquence, Sermon 156.

[13] The Peak of Eloquence, Sayings and Speeches, Hadith number 374.

was to watch over his nation, teach it where it is ignorant, deepen its awareness, and enliven the religious laws in the consciousness and life of his people.

* Second, he had a personal mission. His personal mission was in struggling in the face of internal and external, political and ideological, issues in his community. The Imam (a) was facing an extreme situation in his community. That extremity could not be overcome without making each person in that community, especially the elite, adopt the awareness and practice of enjoining good and forbidding evil. He desired for them to engage so in every necessary situation, especially the dangerous ones.

The Imam (a) was critical of the elite in his community. He condemned them for their corruption, as they were not committed to the causes of their people and homeland. Instead, many of the elite had abandoned those noble causes in pursuit of personal unethical aspiration.

He reprimanded them for their treason, given their betrayal to their people and their cause. Their betrayal is manifested in their abandonment, with no reason, of their duty to enjoin good and forbid evil.

Imam Ali (a) found the elite persistent in their ways and his advice fell on deaf ears. He turned directly to the people in an attempt to motivate them to functionally commit to this principle of enjoining good and forbidding evil. He warned the people of the future threats and aspirations of the elite.

We find the approach of directly addressing the general public in his sermon al-Qasse'a. The sermon was characteristic of various fiery warnings about falling into the traps of the elite. The issue of enjoining good and forbidding evil and the apparent nonchalance of the elite towards this issue were among the most persistent and most dangerous on the Imam's mind.

The Imam used examining history as one of the means to warn his people and to teach them the intellectual value of this duty. His grievances and warnings, characterized by pain and agony, were a result of his harsh daily suffering, from his community in general and from the elite in particular.

Undoubtedly, both groups repeatedly heard the Imam's (a) grievances, as he did in the following example, during his speeches about the people who confront the rulers and are not qualified to do so:

> *I complain to God about persons who live ignorant and die misguided. For them nothing is more worthless than the Qur'an if it is recited as it should be recited, nor anything more valuable than the Qur'an if its verses are*

removed from their places, nor anything more vicious than virtue nor more virtuous than vice.[14]

The Imam (a) ruled by the way of Islam. This approach took into consideration the dignity, prosperity and freedom of the general public. It honored the people's needs and rights. However, this approach was naturally at odds with the interests of the elite and the tribal ruling class who were used to enjoying a host of benefits in the time before Ali's (a) caliphate. This privileged class of people had great influence and used various methods to prevent the Imam (a) from rising to power after the deaths of the Prophet (s), Abu Bakr, and Omar. Nonetheless, Imam Ali (a) assumed power after the passing of Othman in spite of this ruling class. That class of people begrudgingly accepted him due to the pressure of the overwhelming majority of Muslims. That pressure had neutralized the overpowering ability of the financial and influential elite in impacting current events. And so, they adapted to the new situation which brought the long-awaited rule of Imam Ali (a).

Future events would reveal that this adjustment was temporary with the hopes of finding tricks later on that would secure their interests and privileges.

---

[14] The Peak of Eloquence, Sermon 17.

At some point, the elite gave up on the possibility of influencing the Imam (a) to change his leadership approach and policies so that they are aligned with their own interests. They wished to preserve their old positions, get appointed to new positions, and be granted more power and influence over the people in the cities and the rural areas of the nation. When this class despaired and lost hope in bending Ali's (a) firm principles, many of them turned to Syria and Muawiya ibn Abi Sufyan. They saw that his approach and style in dealing with people like themselves were consistent with their understanding and interests. Some of them became derelict in carrying out their military duties in the face of increased military activity from the Kharijites in Syria. Towards the end, these activities were more like quick raids and guerrilla warfare.

This dereliction could not be attributed to cowardliness for their courage was never in doubt. It could also not be attributed to their small numbers since the nation was able to supply its government with vast, strong and well-trained armies who through their nature, culture and conquests over many years rendered them among the finest fighters in the world.

It could also not be justified by a shortage of armament, or lack of preparedness for war and its needs because weapons factories were working in high gear to secure vast reserves of weapons for a nation still at war. Nor can it be justified by a bad economic situation because money was plentiful after the treasury was overhauled during Imam Ali's (a) caliphate.

Therefore, there was no good reason for that dereliction other than an undeclared political position by the elite of the notables and tribal leaders. They persisted in those behaviors until the end with the goal of taking power away from Imam Ali's (a) government, rendering it incapable of effectiveness lacking the necessary means, which would ultimately lead to the triumph of rebellion over legitimacy.

This political position was not only undeclared, but the leaders of this group implied their loyalty and dedication because they feared the general population's judgement and punishment if their true position, intentions, objectives and shameful aspirations became known.

Al-Radi preserved many texts in the Peak of Eloquence where the Imam strongly chastised the elite in his community for their dereliction in their military duties of defending the religion. Toward the end of his rule, no doubt the Imam was compelled to intensify that blame and rebuke, such as when he said:

> *Beware! I called you (insistently) to fight these people night and day, secretly and openly and exhorted you to attack them before they attacked you, because by God, no people have been attacked in the hearts of their houses but they suffered disgrace; but you put it off to others and forsook it until destruction befell you and your cities were occupied...*

How strange! How strange! By God my heart sinks to see the unity of these people on their wrong and your dispersion from your right. Woe and grief befall you. You have become the target at which arrows are shot. You are being killed and you do not kill. You are being attacked but you do not attack. God is being disobeyed and you remain agreeable to it.

When I ask you to move against them in summer you say it is hot weather. Spare us until heat subsides from us. When I order you to march in winter you say it is severely cold; give us time until cold clears from us. These are just excuses for evading heat and cold because if you run away from heat and cold, you would be, by God, running away (in a greater degree) from sword (war).

O you semblance of men, not men, your intelligence is that of children and your wit is that of the occupants of the curtained canopies (women kept in seclusion from the outside world). I wish I had not seen you nor known you. By God, this acquaintance has brought about shame and resulted in repentance. May God fight you! You have filled my heart with pus and loaded my bosom with rage. You made me drink mouthful of grief one after the other.

You shattered my counsel by disobeying and leaving me so much so that Quraysh started saying that the son of Abi Talib is brave but does not know (tactics of) war. God bless them! Is any one of them fiercer in war and older in

it than I am? I rose for it although yet within twenties,
and here I am, have crossed over sixty, but one who is not
obeyed can have no opinion.[15]

* * *

The Imam (a) confronted the elite who were derelict in their duties and betrayed the cause of their people with this level of bitterness, anger, contempt and ridicule.

It would seem that this group or at least some of them, in an effort to conceal their position, which the Imam (a) was exposing, would sometimes feign religious ardor and devotion. They would assume positions of enjoining good and forbidding evil without actually corroborating those positions with action and practices. This was not unlike many others who cover up their treason, selfishness and eagerness for temporal pleasures with only lip service to morals and ethics.

Imam Ali (a), however, recognized those people, and they are easy to recognize in every era. He would harshly expose their deceitful positions because in addition to theirs being crimes of political treason, they were also crimes of deceit and hypocrisy against ordinary people. In helping his community see the corruption of the elite, he said:

---

[15] The Peak of Eloquence, Sermon 27.

Have you not been left among people who are just like rubbish and so low that lips avoid mention of them and do not move even to condemn their low position.

'Verily we are God's and verily unto Him shall we return.'[16]

'Mischief has appeared...'[17] and there is no one to oppose and change it, nor anyone to dissuade from it or desist from it.

Do you, with these qualities, hope to secure abode in the purified neighbourhood of God and to be regarded His staunch lovers? Alas! God cannot be deceived about His paradise and His will cannot be secured save by His obedience. May God curse those who advise good but they themselves avoid it, and those who desist others from evil but they themselves act upon it.[18]

* * *

If the interests of the class or faction-based tyrannical rule require that the people be silent with no objection, protest or condemnation against oppression and violations of rights, then the interests of popular and just rule would be exactly the opposite. It is in the interest of the ruler who draws his effectiveness and strength from the people that the people

---

[16] The Holy Quran, 2:156.
[17] The Holy Quran, 30:41.
[18] The Peak of Eloquence, Sermon 129.

speak up regarding political affairs, in support or criticism in order to protect their true interests from the elite in society. That elite may be undertaking policies that oppose the interests of the people in the short or long term. They may be continuously working on distracting the people from their core interests for other pursuits.[19] This is assuming that the elite had not misled the people and succeeded in turning some of them against just rule.

The silence or indifference of the people in the face the elites' hostile activities leaves the path clear for these forces to corrupt the future policies of the popular rule with no concern for consequences. In such circumstances, the ruler stands unarmed in the face of these forces, preventing them from prevailing. This happened frequently in the time of Imam Ali and the corruption of the elite would anger him and compel him to expose their faults to the people.

Still, Imam Ali (a) was always very careful to move the masses to express their opinion and declare their positions. It is clear to us through texts that the Imam recognized the great and critical importance of this issue on his political career. This was evident in two ways:

---

[19]The Caliphate Othman ibn Affan held a conference with the governors and the elite to address the volatile situation against the government's policies when the waves of protests and complaints grew. The governor of Basra, Abdullah ibn Amer suggested that the armies be trapped where they were (Tjmr) and that they not be permitted to return in order to occupy them with problems from their daily lives instead of political activism. Unfortunately, this suggestion was carried out which led to major discord.

* First: The Imam (a) frequently and in many ways raised the issue of enjoining good and prohibiting evil. This is remarkable given that the religious laws on this subject are clear in the Holy Quran and the prophetic traditions. In addition, many jurists consider this to be among the necessary and peremptory provisions. This insistence reveals that the Imam (a) was facing a state of negligence from the community in relationship to this law and a state of dereliction in its proper application. This negligence and dereliction prompted him to remind Muslims of this duty as frequently as possible.

* Second: The Imam's vehemence in expressing his thoughts and struggles during his sermons to the Muslims reveals that he was suffering from deep worry and repressed anger as a result of the gross negligence he saw in the community. At times, he would reprimand the people and at other times he would encourage and urge them to fulfill this obligation.

* * *

The Imam (a) urged Muslims to practically commit to the obligation of enjoining good and forbidding evil in their daily lives and their social and political relationships in various ways and perspectives.

Examining history was one of the ways the Imam (a) employed in his ideological and political teaching regarding this obligation. Among his teachings from Al-Qasse'a sermon:

> *Certainly, there are examples before you of God's wrath, punishment, days of tribulations and happenings. Therefore, do not disregard His promises, ignoring His punishment, making light His wrath and not expecting His violence, because God, the Glorified, did not curse the past ages except because they had left off asking others to do good acts and refraining them from bad acts. In fact God cursed the foolish for committing sins and the wise because they gave up refraining others from evils.[20]*

We note that in this text, similar to others, the Imam (a) expresses his thoughts about the complacency and inaction in his community towards this obligation. He does so in a harsh powerful manner that progresses beyond calm advice and into severe warnings of great horrors in the future. He supported his point with a reminder of the fate of the past and the damnation brought by the negligence of this duty and the complacency in fulfilling it.

This damnation is not merely a spiritual punishment in the afterlife; rather it also carries a political connotation. This damnation means being disconnected from God's mercy and

---

[20] The Peak of Eloquence, Sermon 192.

favor. It means the damned will experience political and social calamities leading them to decadence and collapse in the end.

It would seem that the Imam (a) was referring to the Israelites when he was talking about the past because his words are inspired from the following verse:

> *Those who disbelieved from among the children of Israel were cursed by the tongue of Dawood and Isa, son of Mariam; this was because they disobeyed and used to exceed the limit. They used not to forbid each other the hateful things (which) they did; certainly evil was that which they did.*[21]

* * *

The Imam (a) also employed his historical analysis on the subject of enjoining good and forbidding evil in the text below. He recounts to his audience the story of the people of Thamud from the Quran and the horrific disaster that led to their demise when they disobeyed God's orders about Prophet Saleh's camel.

Examining a historical Quranic incident is not our primary concern here but rather we wish to further demonstrate the Imam's (a) usage of history in his intellectual teachings.

---

[21] The Holy Quran, 5: 78-79.

The Imam (a) raises an issue of paramount importance in political work through his choice of text. He makes the point that history is impacted by a small group of people with the ability for activism and who take positions while other people remain complacent. By taking positions and acting, this group creates new realities forcing people to accept them and putting the leadership in a position of fait accompli.

When this small group of active people is committed to the issues of their communities and work to achieve their interests, it is incumbent on society to support them morally and materially. However, when this group works against the truth and the communities' overall goals, regardless of the deceit they use to cover up their work, then it is incumbent on society to act and confront them in order to defend those interests.

The community's silence, complacency and passiveness towards this group's positions are a crime they commit against themselves. When disaster strikes as a result of this group's work, it will not distinguish between those who caused it and those who remained quiet. When disaster strikes, its negative effects will impact all of the community and could perhaps impact the silent ones more than the ones who acted, especially in political and ideological issues; because after all, deviance and fraud support the interests of that minority.

Hence we arrive at the modern day term of "the silent majority" in political discourse. This majority does not show interest in what happens around it, or to it, and does not examine those occurring events. Instead the silent majority accepts the actions of others, regardless of whether they are doing so by choice or force. Their acceptance is also regardless of their content or frustration with those events. This silent majority constructively turns its back on justice and becomes an accomplice to the crimes committed. This is because silence in these cases is not a sign of innocence and good-heartedness; rather, it is a sign of cowardice, negligence and evading responsibility.

This complacency that rises to the level of the crime itself is not absolved from punishment. And the punishment in this case is not enforced by the authorities since it is society's laws that caused the disaster in the first place. This punishment does not distinguish between the complacent and the one who acted, rather it sweeps everyone away. This punishment is vetted out by God Almighty who chastises all for their sins: those who acted and committed the crime and those who were silent on account that they provided the environment for that crime and for those who committed it.

Therefore, from this perspective, the silent majority does not consist of any innocent bystanders; instead it involves accomplices and cowards who took part in laying the groundwork for future misfortune by favoring their own immediate personal safety. Their cowardice, which exposes their shameful and humiliating selfishness, also reveals that they are not a solid generation that can build a prosperous life.

Social disasters are like natural disasters – they wash away both the venomous and the beneficial plants, not distinguishing between them in the destruction.

The Imam (a) said:

> *O people, certainly, what gathers people together (in categories) is (their) agreement (to good or bad) and (their) disagreement, for only one individual killed the camel of Thamud but God held all of them in punishment because all of them consented to it.*[22]

* * *

In one of his sessions discussing the future, the Imam (a) warned the people about an ideological and cultural state that leads to abandoning the underlying tenets of the Islamic community. These tenets distinguish the community from all others and give it a unique role in impacting history and building civilization. Abandoning these tenets makes this culture another one of many. It renders the cultural structure derived from the Holy Book and prophetic traditions merely superficial practice and ritual. It loses the depth of concepts, building character and forging a way forward.

---

[22] The Peak of Eloquence, Sermon 201.

Muslims in the case above would be forsaking their Holy Book as a source for ideological concepts. They would consequently be turning to sources strange to their own culture, civilization, beliefs, religious laws, and history to obtain behavioral guidance and intellectual and psychological sustenance.

It is important to note here that interacting with other cultures is different from abandoning one's own culture. Interacting and being open to other cultures with the aspirations of discovering other cultures and their intellectual achievements, while preserving one's own essence and remaining faithful to one's own tenets, is desired and required in Islam. In fact, Muslims had practiced this behavior and mastered it when they established the great Islamic civilization. This civilization discovered and adapted other civilizations to the Islamic values, notions and ethics which were all derived from the Holy Book, prophetic traditions and jurisprudence.

The Imam (a) said:

> *Certainly, a time will come upon you after me when nothing will be more concealed than rightfulness, nothing more apparent than wrongfulness and nothing more current than untruth against God and His Prophet. For the people of this period nothing will be more valueless than the Qur'an being recited as it ought to be recited, nor anything more valuable than the Qur'an being misplaced from its position. And in the towns nothing will be more*

hated than virtue, nor anything more acceptable than vice. The holders of the book will throw it away and its memorizers would forget it. In these days the Qur'an and its people will be exiled and expelled. They will be companions keeping together on one path, but no one will offer them asylum. Consequently at this time the Qur'an and its people will be among the people but not among them, will be with them but not with them, because misguidance cannot accord with guidance even though they may be together.[23]

The last paragraph above clearly depicts the reality of separation between a nation and its ideological leadership as a result of abandoning one's own culture and moving away from its ideological concepts and guidance.

This cultural "alienation," resulting from the abandonment of one's own beliefs and not from interacting with others, leads to a dangerous situation as related to good and evil. There are two measures of moral values and ideals; one is objective and the other is arbitrary.

The objective measure is one that draws its moral values from the faith and its laws. For example, in Islam moral values are drawn from the Islamic faith and laws. Such would be the case for Christianity or Buddhism as well.

---

[23] The Peak of Eloquence, Sermon 147.

This measure requires that the community is committed to its faith and laws manifested in its institutions, systems and relationships. Such commitment would need to reflect to a point where the community itself is an expression of that faith and its laws.

The arbitrary measure is one that makes the person himself the source of moral values. In this case, the person establishes the ethics and values that adapt his behavior towards society and his relationships within society. This measure excludes any external sources for ethics and values.

It is then that conflict occurs between the official doctrine and its laws on the one hand and the ethics and values of its individuals and groups on the other. For example, in Muslim, Christian or Buddhist societies, when arbitrariness is prevalent, we will undoubtedly discover that the community's commitment to its beliefs and its laws are only superficial and are accompanied by practical atheism.

The impact of an objective measure versus an arbitrary one, with regards to commitment to values in society, is extremely important.

First, adopting an objective measure leads to growth in the individual without unnecessary complexities or internal conflict. This is because it provides uniformity and integration between the conscience, the mind, and behavioral expressions within and outside the community.

On the other hand, adopting an arbitrary measure leads to the opposite of the above. An arbitrary measure leads the individual to unnecessary complexities and internal conflict because it constantly gears him toward contradiction. He is torn between personal desires as a source of value on one hand and complying with the beliefs and its laws on the other. This leads to harmful repercussions that impact not only the individual but the collective community as well.

Second, through the homogeneity provided between ethics, beliefs and its law, an objective measure leads to widespread cohesion within the community. It also unifies the community's view of the problems it faces. In addition, it draws closer the positions of diverse groups regarding the challenges in their community.

Arbitrariness causes the opposite effect. It leads to instability in the social structure and to various competing intellectual and political groups. It generates an environment suitable for rise of social problems because the nature of arbitrary measures is that vary significantly from one individual to the next.

This fragmentation leads to an inability to take common positions on a national or community level because of the diversity in wills and preferences. Likewise it could lead to a surrendering of the masses to the political will, convictions and beliefs of the select few with self-serving objectives. These select few force the larger groups to accept choices in conflict with the true interests of the nation but in line with the interest of that group which has the means for propaganda and media. This is occurring in modern times and is leading to major disasters at the national level in some cases and at the global level in others. Regional peace, and world peace for that matter, is subjected to the aspirations and ambitions of a select few impacting the minds of entire peoples. Such influence constructively drives the masses to take political positions that are in conflict with their national interests and the interests of the people. The Palestinian situation is the greatest example of this.

Imam Ali warned of this danger and cautioned his community against it saying:

> *I wonder, and there is no reason why I should not wonder, about the faults of these groups who have introduced alterations in their religious pleas, who do not move on the footsteps of their Prophet nor follow the actions of the vicegerent. They do not believe in the unknown and do not avoid the evil. They act on the doubts and tread in (the way of) their passions. For them good is whatever they consider good and evil is whatever they consider evil.*
>
> *Their reliance for resolving distresses is on themselves. Their confidence in regard to dubious matters is on their own opinions as if every one of them is the Leader (Imam) of himself. Whatever he has decided himself he*

considers it to have been taken through reliable sources and strong factors.[24]

* * *

And finally, to emphasize the importance of the obligation of enjoining good and forbidding evil, Imam Ali (a) made it a prominent and important part of his will to his sons Imams Hassan (a) and Hussain (a).

The Imam (a) repeated this part of his will twice. The first was to his son Imam Hassan (a) in the encompassing will he wrote in front of witnesses when he was leaving for Siffin. The second was to Imam Hassan (a) and Hussain (a) on his deathbed after he was struck by the sword of Ibn Muljem al-Muradi.

He (a) said in the first will:

> *... Ask others to do good; you will thus be among good doers. Desist others from evil with your action as well as speech and keep off, to the best of your ability, from he who commits it. Struggle for God as is His due; and the insults of a reviler should not stop you in matters of God.[25]*

And he (a) said in his second will:

---

[24] The Peak of Eloquence, Sermon 88.

[25] The Peak of Eloquence, Hadith number 31.

... I advise you (both) and all my children and members of my family and everyone whom my writing reaches... You should keep to a respect for kinship and spending for others. Avoid turning away from one another and severing mutual relations. Do not give up bidding for good and forbidding from evil lest the mischievous gain positions over you, and then if you will pray, the prayers will not be granted.[26]

* * *

God's blessings upon Ali ibn Abi Talib (a) forever and always

---

[26] The Peak of Eloquence, Hadith number 47.

PART III
HISTORY AND POLITICS

INTRODUCTION

The Imam was a politician. His political demeanor was that of a statesman. He was a true visionary. Political work consumed his life during the lifetime of the Prophet (s). The Prophet (s) assigned him in various capacities and roles. The Imam's (a) political leadership continued during the reign of the caliphs who came before him, due to their need for him and the need of people. In addition, he was a ruler and a head of state in the later years of his life.

In light of these two considerations, the Imam was constantly needed to give the necessary political direction to his nation and his aides. At times, when providing such direction, he would use historical references to highlight the political idea he was proposing. He would give his political guidance practical relevance in addition to his proposed theoretical assessment... The practical credibility added warmth and allure to his political guidance. Through this approach, the Imam "humanized" his political guidance and positioned it so it engages the heart just as it guides the mind.

Policy for a man of the religion and a ruler of a nation, like Imam Ali (a) the Commander of the Faithful, is an instrument to overcome the negativity of the past. It is a tool to triumph in the present in order to attain better conditions in the future for the largest proportion of people.

At the same time, policy is a tool to maintain the positive aspects of the past and the present in the face of the turmoil of change and sudden instabilities that could bring disaster to the political community. Hence, policy is not only the art of change but it is also the art of consistency.

A politician who is faithful to the issues of his community lives in all of the dimensions of time: past, present and future. He deals with the facts from the past, the reality of the present and the hopes, fears and aspirations of the future. He leads his community towards new horizons with caution without rigidity, and risk-taking without recklessness. He does this without curtailing its continuity or distance from the past.

We say this in the face of the advocates of change in present day; the change which aims to eradicate our roots in order to hurl us into an emptiness under the banner of leading the future. This kind of change makes us the field of experimentation for the theories and ideas present in modern day centers of civilization in Europe, the United States and Russia.

We say this to call for a second look at this attitude for the sake of another approach that is less radical. This is for the sake of an approach that is more realistic and better connected with our religious, civilization and cultural make-up. That approach is also more in harmony with our interests in the present and the future. It is more satisfactory to regaining our role through which we aspire to contribute to save modern man by putting modern civilization to rights and correcting its course towards a suitable status.

* * *

As we will see in the following chapters, Imam Ali's (a) policies were obsessed with one great and noble goal: the creation of a complete, strong and happy Muslim person and the creation of a complete, strong and happy Muslim society. This person and that society would be qualified to be a force of good in the world and would represent the permanent and glowing human ambition towards betterment.

As such, this policy did not derive its characteristics from self-preservation or the preservation of the interests of the ruler and his family; the Imam's (a) family was the most deprived of the bounties of his reign and he was most deprived among his family.

His policies were enlightened with intellect and guided by the teachings of God. They were based in the values of ethics and virtues that would honor man. As such, the Imam's (a) policies were humanitarian to the full meaning of the word.

His policies were never a series of actions and reactions or tallying up profits and losses for himself, his family and inner circle. Those sort of policies carry the spirit of recklessness and instinct, guided by a temperamental mentality of means and commerce.

Imam Ali's policies were faithful to his religion and its laws, never deviating from them or transcending them or slacking in his duties towards anything or any situation.

Being faithful to his Quranic and prophetic ethics, Imam Ali (a) transformed his political work into an exercise of virtues. He was faithful to his community and his virtues were partner to his decision-making after showing it the consequences of bad choices:

> We are in a period when most of the people regard betrayal as wisdom. In these days the ignorants call it excellence of cunning. What is the matter with them? God may destroy them.
> One who has been through thick and thin of life finds the excuses to be preventing him from orders and prohibitions of God but he disregards them despite capability (to succumb to them and follows the commands of God), while one who has no restraints of religion seizes the

opportunity (and accepts the excuses for not following the commands of God).[1]

He said in another situation:

By God, Mu`awiyah is not more cunning than I am, but he deceives and commits evil deeds. Had it not been for the reprehensibility of deceit, I would have been the most cunning of all men. But (the fact is that) every deceit is a sin and every sin is disobedience (of God), and every deceitful person will have a banner by which he will be recognised on the Day of Judgement. By God, I cannot be made forgetful by strategy, nor can I be overpowered by hardships.[2]

* * *

After this preface, we will next cover how the Commander of the Faithful Ali bin Abi Talib dealt with history in his political teachings.

---

[1] The Peak of Eloquence, Sermon 41.

[2] The Peak of Eloquence, Sermon 200.

REVOLUTION AND SOCIETY

Humans are always moving in time and space. They innovate and communicate through trade and friendship, at times, and through hostility and war, at other times. But they consistently innovate and communicate through ideologies. They also always interact with nature; they adjust it and adapt to it. They love it and at times, they run away from it.

Sometimes they face failures and disappointments and other times, they are elated from the ecstasy of victory. At times, they are paralyzed from despair, but soon thereafter, hope for prosperity and advancement ignites the flame of desire for change in their hearts and so they start moving again.

Thus humans are always making their own history. They weave it thread by thread and build it atom by atom from the millions of small hopes, fears, envies, and desires which altogether make the crux of history.

However, they will not become history if they did not take on a certain frame or if they do not get formed in a particular manner... that is if they did not include the idea of change, the spirit of change, and the determination to change. These will transform the millions of individual hopes and fears into one big pulsating spirit engulfing society and its people with its glow. It will push them forward as one unified and vibrant movement, rather than scattered individual paths. They will have one vision or multiple converging visions for change. Only then will the calm and peaceful movement of history be built, become great, give birth to significant events and put society and the people at a new juncture in history.

This interaction may occur at times of peace and social stability causing the period of change, after a period of preparation, to be relatively longer. That is because in these cases, changes in history happen in accordance with the notions of peace and stability which make a person more careful and patient in his movement and as such better able to choose.

In cases where this interaction occurs in states of social upheaval and widespread apprehension, two different phenomena arise:

- The phenomenon of rejection and rebellion among the masses fed and fueled by despair from the formal state of justice. Hope for a better future enlivens the masses through the advocates of change.

- The phenomenon of repression used by the authorities in order to ensure the sovereignty and stability of their rule and values.

This repression strengthens the feelings of despair and anger, and it causes more rebellion and rejection. It causes stress to a higher degree of rigidity and structure for millions of hopes, fears, hatreds and desires. It fuels anger and pushes the masses further and further to violence in order to get on a path of change.

In this case, the crucial period for change to take hold is shortened, following a period of preparation. Events would accelerate and grow in size and the geography of the participating groups expands. Events escalate to a climax where the prevailing era collapses and society enters a new period of history.

* * *

Humans do not stop making history; they may make their own history in times of peace, times of turmoil and social unrest or times of war.

Imam Ali (a) noted that history was being made under the second set of conditions [times of turmoil and social unrest] because the prevailing conditions in society at that time were pushing the community towards a bloody path in the face of a gloomy future, rife with tribulations.

The errors in judgment during the reign of the Caliph Othman ibn Affan caused disappointment and anger among many groups of Muslims. In addition, they also caused many of the values, ethics and aspirations of pre-Islamic times to thrive again. This was at the hands of those who believed in them, represented them, and who were at the pinnacle of authority in the political, economic and societal fields. The resurgence of these pre-Islamic values led to conflict between the representatives of these values and the majority of Muslims whose spirits were reassured by the hopes that Islam fosters justice and equality. This tragic conflict was constantly being fueled by the errors of the rulers and the reemerging policies of pre-Islamic times. As such, it became more acute and kept expanding in breadth and scope.

All of the above accumulated over the years and expanded until it included all communities within the nation. Ultimately, it led to its expected severe consequences and bitter end: a revolution by the rich and the poor, the disgruntled without malice, and the haters from among the elite. The revolution led to the murder of the Caliph Uthman and the beginning of a new direction in history for Muslims. They asked Imam Ali (a) to lead them thereafter but he refused their request. Given his awareness of history and its impacts, he knew that the sheer volume of unfulfilled needs and the hopes in people's heart far exceeded the potential abilities of the government's institutions. He also knew that the magnitude of the obstacles represented by the symbols of the bygone era and its forces is large and dangerous because even though they were paralyzed by the revolution, they were still ingrained in all of the centers of powers. Declaring his refusal, the Imam (a) said to the people:

> *Leave me and seek some one else. We are facing a matter that has (several) faces and colors, which neither hearts can stand nor intelligence can accept. Clouds are hovering over the sky, and faces are not discernible. You should know that if I respond to you I would lead you as I know and would not listen to the utterance of any speaker or the reproof of any reprover. If you leave me then I am the same as you are. It is possible I would listen to and obey whomever you make in charge of your affairs. I am better for you as a counsellor than as chief.[1]*

The Imam (a) would remind the people of his position on many occasions, including his words when Talha and Zubair came to fight him:

> *You advanced towards me shouting "allegiance, allegiance" like she-camels having delivered newly born young ones leaping towards their young. I held back my*

---

[1] The Peak of Eloquence, Sermon 92.

hand but you pulled it towards you. I drew back my hand
but you dragged it.[2]

He also said to Talha and Zubair:

By God, I had no liking for the caliphate nor any interest
in government, but you yourselves invited me to it and
prepared me for it...[3]

And he said on another occasion:

... You drew out my hand towards you for allegiance but
I held it back and you stretched it but I contracted it.
Then you crowed over me as the thirsty camels crowd on
the watering cisterns on their being taken there, so much
so that shoes were torn, shoulder-cloths fell away and the
weak got trampled, and the happiness of people on their
allegiance to me was so manifested that small children felt
joyful, the old staggered (up to me) for it, the sick too
reached for it helter skelter and young girls ran for it
without veils.[4]

Why did Ali bin Abi Talib (a) refuse?

Perhaps he had hoped that after society experienced turmoil
and upheaval in the prior era, it would experience a period of

---

[2] The Peak of Eloquence, Sermon 137.

[3] The Peak of Eloquence, Sermon 205.

[4] The Peak of Eloquence, Sermon 228.

transition led by men against whom the new powers, represented by the pre-Islamic values, would not rebel.

However, desire was overwhelming, as reflected in the above-mentioned texts and it was not possible to transfer the allegiance and trust of the people to an alternative. Refusal would have spelled disaster because the pre-Islamic forces were capable of returning after re-gathering their strengths if the void in authority continued. In such case, the Islamic community would have been deprived of an experience that would become a model and a source of inspiration in the future.

There is no shortage of texts in the Peak of Eloquence that shed light on this issue and strongly suggest that the Imam (a) was thinking along those lines. An example of this is shown through his words in a speech that the Sharif Al-Radi titled "He revealed his reasons for wanting to govern and described the true Imam:"

> ... O my God! Thou knowest that what we did was not to seek power nor to acquire anything from the vanities of the world. We rather wanted to restore the signs of Thy religion and to usher prosperity into Thy cities so that the oppressed among Thy creatures might be safe and Thy forsaken commands might be established.[5]

---

[5] The Peak of Eloquence, Sermon 131.

Another example is a letter the Imam (a) wrote to Malik Al-Ashtar, after assigning him as the governor of Egypt:

> ... *But I am worried that foolish and wicked people will control the affairs of the entire community, with the result that they will grab the funds of God as their own property and make His people slaves, fight with the virtuous, and ally with the sinful...*[6]

And so it was that the Imam responded to the urgent and eager wishes and, as it seems, reluctantly accepted to assume power and lead the nation. Three political-ideological forces crystallized and were determined through his acceptance to assume office:

The pure prophetic Islamic force: This was represented by the legitimate authority (the Caliphate), led by the Commander of the Faithful Ali bin Abi Talib (a).

The immediate and direct goal of this force was to correct the political, administrative, and economic conditions in the Muslim society which was eagerly looking forward to changes that would achieve its hopes. This goal had an underlying motive and that is to restore the theoretical and practical considerations to the Islamic values and concepts.

The pre-Islamic force pretending to be Islamic: This force enjoyed broad and established authority in the Syrian region. It

---

[6] The Peak of Eloquence, Letters and Sayings, Letter number 62.

also had pockets of authority in Hijaz, Iraq and Egypt among other Muslim countries.

From the very first moments, it seemed that the leader of this force was Muawiya ibn Abi Sufyan. Also, that the immediate and ultimate goal of this force was to reestablish the old conditions and to cause the prophetic forces to fail or to at least suppress them by causing them problems and tribulations.

It was the counter-revolution. It was a means to stem the wave of change.

The Imam expressed his views of the leaders of this force that they "intend reverting the matters on their backs (pre-Islamic period)" as part of his speech to the people of Jamel:

> Certainly, these people are in agreement in disliking my authority. I will carry on until I perceive disunity among you; because if, in spite of the unsoundness of their view, they succeed, the whole organization of the Muslims will be shattered. They are hankering after this world out of jealousy against him on whom God has bestowed it. So they intend reverting the matters on their backs (pre-Islamic period), while on us it is obligatory, for your sake, to abide by the Book of God (Qur'an), the Sublime, and the conduct of the Prophet of God, to stand by His rights and the revival of his sunnah.[7]

---

[7] The Peak of Eloquence, Sermon 169.

The force of the confused and the hesitant: If hesitation can be called a force or an approach.

This force was represented by some secondary leaders, including Saad ibn Abi Waqqas, Abdallah ibn Omar and others.

This force did not reach enough clarity or awareness so it can be counted within the prophetic forces. The interests of its members were on one side while the effects of piety in the souls of some of its members were on the other side. Some of these men took caution from the pre-Islamic approach and so they did not align themselves with it at this stage, although later on, some of them ended up aligned with that approach.

Imam Ali (a) said about them: "They abandoned right but did not support wrong."[8]

> *It is said that Al-Harith ibn Hawt came to the Commander of the Faithful, and said: Do you believe I can ever imagine that the people of Jamel were in the wrong? The Commander of the Faithful, peace be upon him, said: O Al-Harith! You have seen below yourself but not above yourself, and so you have been confused. Certainly, you have not known right, so that you can recognize the righteous. And you have not known wrong, so that you can recognize the people of wrong! Then Al-*

---

[8] The Peak of Eloquence, Letters and Sayings, Hadith number 18.

176

*Harith said: In that case, I shall withdraw along with
Sa'd ibn Malik and 'Abdullah: ibn 'Umar; whereupon the
Commander of the Faithful, peace be upon him, said:
Verily, Sa'd and 'Umar have neither sided with Right
nor forsaken Wrong.[9]*

Some of the followers of this position enjoyed limited respect
in their tribal bases. This respect did not stem from ideological
loyalty but rather from a tribal one. They also enjoyed limited
respect from Muslim masses stemming from their friendship
with the Prophet (a) and from the obscurity of their position
from the available choices in the political arena.

* * *

Imam Ali (a) realized the difficulty of his position from the
very beginning. Thus, he told the nation that its movement has
reacquired a pre-Islamic quality, the same as it had been before
the Prophet. He also was honest with the nation that
confronting these revitalized and obsolete values will require
strong and stringent rule. In addition, he told them that the
hopes for a quick and complete change for the better need to be
somewhat cohesive in order to allow the legitimate authority to
confront the pre-Islamic forces with flexibility.

The Imam (a) expressed this political vision in a sermon he
delivered at the beginning of his caliphate in Medina. In his

---

[9] The Peak of Eloquence, Letters and Sayings, Hadith number 262.

book "Al-Bayan wa al-Tabyeen", Al-Jaheth relates from Abi Obeida Muammar Al-Muthanna, that the Imam (a) said:

> *Do not be content with yourself. He who has heaven and hell in his view has no other aim. He who attempts and acts quickly, succeeds, while the seeker who is slow may also entertain hope, and he who falls short of action faces destruction in Hell... On right and left there are misleading paths. Only the middle way is the (right) path which is the Everlasting Book and the traditions of the Prophet. God has medicated this nation with two forms of treatment: the whip and the sword. The Imam cannot be lenient with the use of either. Hide yourselves in your homes[10] and reform yourselves. Repentance is at your back.[11]*

At first he warned them of inciting instability and unrest. He then brought to the forefront of their minds and hearts the reality of afterlife and the Day of Judgment. Then, he showed them that deviating from the approach of the Quran and Tradition of the Prophet (s) in either direction would lead to misguidance and aberrance, and as such the resurging pre-Islamic approach would lead people astray.

---

[10] Hide yourselves in your homes: He is not referring to mandated curfews.

[11] The Peak of Eloquence, Sermon 16.Ibn Abi Hadid, Shareh Nahj Al-Balagha 1/ 275-276. Sharif al-Radi recounted this sermon with modifications to some of the expression, see Sermon 176: "From his sermon about martyrdom and piety." It is believed that he said this sermon after Othman was killed at the beginning of his Caliphate.

And then he revealed to them that the upcoming phase in rule had to be strict ("using the whip and the sword"). Therefore, people should not engage in anything that would make the situation worse by inciting tribal prejudices and clan tendencies. He called on them to stop and repent from the prior actions of deviation.

After that, he gave them the right to hold him accountable and he demanded his right for their support and allegiance. He went on to express his foretelling of the gloom of the future and his doubt about the prophetic approach regaining its previous power. However, in spite of that, he did not lose hope that the situation would improve.

He warned them that the bright hopes of change for the better, back to the pure prophetic approach, need a show of solidarity among themselves. He noted that those who hold such hopes had to once again be realistic in their expectations.

Ibn Abi Hadid said in explaining this section:

> The 'period' is the time between prophets when there are no apostles, such as the period between Jesus (a) and Muhammad (s). There was no prophet in between them, unlike the period between Moses and Jesus, when there were many prophets... It was as if he knew that matters will become unstable... He is saying that I am doing what is required of me in upholding the laws of the religion and keeping away from the Muslims the corrupt

governors and princes. If what I desire is achieved then be it, otherwise, I have my excuses.[12]

* * *

Therefore, the Imam (a) accepted power while having a mix of pessimism and hope. However, soon thereafter, the flames of hope started to wane. On one hand, the hesitant parties quickly started taking the side of the camp in alliance with the prophetic approach, at least in secret if not openly. On the other hand, the angry populace, whose hearts were filled with hopes for change just for the sake of change without regard to the current conditions, started leaning towards the opposing rebellion. It was vital to have a balanced approach in order to avoid internal strife in the community which could lead to changes in the immature forces allied with the prophetic approach.

* * *

Thus, after the shock that crippled the forces of the opposing revolution and after the waiting period experienced by other parties in the nation, the situation exploded yet another time and the community was once again roiled. Unrest and hectic turmoil returned.

At this point, when the crisis in governance and ideology peaked, the landmarks of the future history of the Islamic

---

[12] Ibn Abi Hadid, Shareh Nahj Al-Balagha 1/ 281.

nation became very painfully clear to the Imam. It would be a future full of horrors and tragedies. It would be characteristic of bleakness, blood, rifts, and collapses, occasionally punctuated with glimmers of hope and fleeting moments of peace but with definite cruel disappointments.

With intuition guided by prophetic direction and a mind that understands the impacts and mechanisms of history, the Imam saw the approaching strife with all of the darkness, tricks and its casting of falsehood with truth. He also saw after that the victory of apostasy with its pre-Islamic values donning Islam (like wearing a fur inside out).

And he saw the suffering of the nation: he heard with his big heart the cries of the oppressed who were crushed by the brutal fangs of struggle. He also saw the bloodshed of the victims. By his humanity, his dignity, and his ever encompassing heart, he felt the humiliation of the Muslim person in an apostate society. He cried bitterly for all that would befall his people after him.

And he saw after that the fire of revolution burning and destroying everything, feeding on the hatred and bitterness of the people. However, this revolution would be victim to the errors of sedition at times and would fall into the traps of sedition at other times and would seldom take the middle path.

Finally, he saw, in the very distant future, and after lots of torment and struggling, the light of hope that would come in the end... the light of salvation.

SEDITION

Sedition is a Quranic expression that, when assigned to God or by Him, sometimes means Divine trials and tests. Among related verses are the Almighty's sayings:

> *And know that your property and your children are a temptation, and that God is He with Whom there is a mighty reward.*[1]

There are other sources related to Divine trials and tests through difficulties and tribulations. The following verse is another example:

> *Do men think that they will be left alone on saying, We believe, and not be tried? And certainly We tried those before them, so God will certainly know those who are true and He will certainly know the liars.*[2]

---

[1] The Holy Quran, 8:28. Another similar verse occurs at 64:15.

[2] The Holy Quran, 29:2-3.

These seditions have a pedagogical role which strengthens the believers, enhances their awareness and distinguishes them from the intruders and the hypocrites.

This Quranic expression with its positive pedagogical meaning became a political and historical term for Imam Ali. It had a variety of connotations linked to the impact of history in community both in the present and the future. It had a negative connotation for the progressive prophetic approach.

The Imam considered sedition, as a political phenomenon, an impediment to progression and a setback in the progress of the prophetic movement. Therefore, it is not brought on by God but rather it is man-made.

* * *

The Imam divided sedition into two parts:

* The first one is the meaning of sedition according to Quranic pedagogical interpretation. He considered sedition in this sense to have positive role, provided man responds to it in a faithful committed spirit and an ethical and responsible awareness. Therefore, there is no point in asking God to forbid this kind of sedition. That would be absurd because this sedition is inherent to the nature of life and man's existence. Life would not be complete without the presence of sedition in this sense.

*   The second is sedition in the political sense. This is the kind about which the Imam warns and from which he seeks refuge. And it is to this sedition that the Imam gave political and historical implications in his teachings. He called them "seditions of deviance."

He explained his perspective by saying:

> *None of you should say, "O God, I seek Your protection from trouble" because there is no one who is not involved in trouble, but whoever seeks God's protection he should seek it from misguiding troubles, because God, the Glorified, says: And know you that your wealth and your children are a temptation!. (Qur'an, 8:28) and its meaning is that He tries people with wealth and progeny in order to distinguish one who is displeased with his livelihood from the one who is happy with what he has been given. Even though God, the Glorified, knows them more than they know themselves yet He does so to let them perform actions with which they earn reward or punishment because some of them like to have male (children) and dislike to have female (children), and some like to amass wealth, and dislike adversity.[3]*

* * *

---

[3] The Peak of Eloquence, Letters and Sayings, Hadith number 93.

The objective of this study is not to research sedition in its pedagogical sense, rather it is to research it as a political and historical term. We will see in the following pages how the Imam divided sedition as a political term and his analysis of its motivations: how it grows, how it spreads and his direction on how to react when it happens. We will also look at Imam Ali's role in confronting the sedition that had begun at the time of his rule and finally we will look at his perspective on the sedition by the Umayyads after his rule.

* * *

It would seem that there are three types of sedition based on analyzing and comparing the different texts in The Peak of Eloquence:

1. Broad sedition.
2. Occasional sedition.
3. Dominant sedition.

These labels were not used by Imam Ali, rather we assigned them based on our observations of the pedagogical impact of sedition and consequently its impact on the political situation and human and social relationships within the community.

BROAD SEDITION

Sedition is broad when it is a prevailing system of ideologies in a civilized or a Bedouin community. A civilization where life is built on delusional values in ideologies, morality and loss, where political and social institutions are established based on those values, and where corrupt relationships control the political environment is in fact a civilization where broad sedition affects every person and its impacts expand beyond its own borders. This would fall in the category of 'pre-Islamic times' regardless of whether it is in the past or present.

This is also the case when such a pedagogical system is the basis for the spirit and mind of a Bedouin society where civilization has not grown to higher levels in interacting with nature and organizational institutions.

Imam Ali characterized this kind of broad sedition in his speech about the state of the world in general, and the Arabs specifically, before the Prophet's message:

> *...I also stand witness that Muhammad (s) is His slave and His prophet. God sent him with the illustrious religion, effective emblem, written Book... At that time people had fallen in vices whereby the rope of religion had been broken, the pillars of belief had been shaken, principles had been sacrileged, system had become topsy turvy, openings were narrow, passage was dark, guidance was unknown and darkness prevailed. God was being disobeyed, Satan was given support and Belief had been forsaken. As a result the pillars of religion fell down, its traces could not be discerned, its passages had been*

destroyed and its streets had fallen into decay. People obeyed Satan and treaded his paths. They sought water from his watering places. Through them Satan's emblems got flying and his standard was raised in vices which trampled the people under their hoofs, and treaded upon them with their feet. The vices stood on their toes (in full stature) and the people immersed in them were strayed, perplexed, ignorant and seduced as though in a good house with bad neighbors. Instead of sleep they had wakefulness and for antimony they had tears in the eyes. They were in a land where the learned were in bridle (keeping their mouths shut) while the ignorant were honored.[4]

In the above text, the Imam laid out his view of one example of sedition as a political phenomenon in society.

The characteristics of sedition based on the above are as follows:

1. It is a society that is not governed by a moral system and it is void from a sound spiritual life. This does not preclude such a society from having a political system.

   The Imam indicates this characteristic by saying "vices whereby the rope of religion had been broken" because this society is not connected to revelation and as such does not benefit from a spiritual and moral system.

---

[4] The Peak of Eloquence, Sermon 2.

2. It is a society whose members and groups are controlled by doubt. A selfish approach is followed in this society because it does not benefit from an objective measure due to the lack of a moral system and a spiritual life.

The Imam indicates this second characteristic when he says in the above text "the pillars of belief had been shaken."

3. This society is divided into parties and factions and is torn by conflicts and disputes which make it void of solidarity and interdependence. As such, its actions are not guided towards common hopes or a grand moral objective. Rather it is driven by individual and factional desires in part because of the absence of moral order and in part because of the spirit of doubt and following one's own scale of values.

The Imam illustrates this characteristic by saying "principles had been sacrileged, system had become topsy turvy, openings were narrow, passage was dark..."

These are the characteristics that distinguish broad sedition and that imprint with their character the affected communities. The above description of society is a result of these three main characteristics:

* Lack of a moral system and spiritual life,

* Being controlled by doubt and using only a selfish scale in assessing values, divisions by class, factions and families, and

* The absence of a grand and noble goal that guides the actions of society.

This is broad sedition. We called it 'broad' because it encompasses all of society without excluding any of its levels or ways of life. It is its spirit and mind… its inspiring spirit and its guiding mind.

OCCASIONAL SEDITION

Sedition is occasional when there is a hindrance in society's progression. Such sedition would cause confusion and ambiguity in some situations, exposure of some of society's leaders and factions to critical tests, and allowing some old values to re-emerge. However, society's progressive momentum and the strength of its guiding principles in the hearts and minds of its people prevent sedition from spreading and taking root in the folds of society. Justice is quickly revealed in those situations and the impact of sedition withers and the voices of its supporters dim and they in fact become subject to criticism and defamation. Then the regressive movements that feed sedition disappear. Society recovers once again from its trials and comes out of that experience with better awareness and alertness.

Muslims experienced some occasional sedition during the time of the Prophet and they successfully overcame them with the Prophet's guidance. They overcame these experiences with no impact on the forward progress of the Muslim community.

Perhaps the most dangerous of these occasional seditions that the Muslim society faced was that of Ifk in the sixth Hijra year upon the Prophet and the Muslims invading the people of Mustaliq from Khouza'a.

Prior to the incident at Ifk, and during the trip back from the aforementioned invasion, there was contention over water at some of the homes on the way. This was between a hired hand for Omar ibn al-Khattab from Bani Ghaffar named Jahjah and an ally of Khazraj named Sinan bin Waber al-Juhani. They fought and the ally of Khazraj cried out, "O Ansar!" and Omar bin al-Khattab's employee cried out "O Mouhajreen!" Hypocrites, led by Abdallah ibn Abi Salool, went to work to exploit the tension resulting from this simple argument between the Ansar and the Mouhajreen. Ibn Abi Salool threatened them that if they returned to the city, "the honored ones would leave humiliated." Sedition was on the verge of affecting many.

However, the Prophet's wisdom prevailed and crushed this sedition before it grew. God revealed the chapter of the Hypocrites (al-Munafiqun) in relation to this passing sedition. In it, He exposed the intents and methods of the hypocrites and He made it an educational lesson in faith and politics for Muslims, helping to deepen their awareness, increase their vigilance and reinforce their strength in the face of such hypocrisies.

The sedition at Ifk was more dangerous and widespread. It was the breeding ground for hypocrites through which they were weakening the status of the Prophet, tarnishing his reputation and casting shadows of suspicion on the purity of his home in a community built on strict values as related to sexual purity. This included all that comes from quiet whispers on such a matter in such a community; ridicule, doubts, and rumors that weakened the psychological impact of the Prophet's directives.

Even more serious than the insinuations of the hypocrites and their exploitation of possibilities provided by Ifk are the cracks in the cohesion of the Muslims themselves. Some leaders of the Aws tribe took advantage of the involvement of some members of the Khazraj tribe in spreading rumors about Ifk to express their own backwards hatred under the guise of caring for the Prophet and adhering to the rules of the religion.

The leader of Aws, Osaid ibn Hadeer, said, without naming anyone, to the Prophet when the latter gently admonished those who were spreading the false rumor:

"O Messenger of God, if they are from Aws, we will stop them. If they are from our brothers of Khazraj, give us your order for by God they deserve to have their heads cut off."

And then Saad ibn Abada, the leader of Khazraj responded to him saying:

"By God, you are lying. You will not cut off their heads. By God, you only said what you said because you knew they were from Khazraj. You would not have said that if they were from among your people…"

Then Osaid ibn Hadeer said:

"By God, you are lying. However you are a hypocrite, arguing for the hypocrites…"

The people argued and were confronting each other, ready to fight until it seemed likely that there will be malignity between these two neighbors.[5] Such did the old pre-Islamic values find an outlet to express themselves through this sedition, under the guise of Islamic values.

However, the Prophet's wisdom, the community's awareness, and the solidity of Islamic values in the minds of the elite confined this sedition to a narrow range and prevented it from negatively impacting the progress of the Prophetic movement. Revelation followed and terminated this sedition when God Almighty revealed the chapter of al-Nur in this regard (chapter 24). He made it an educational lesson that is suitable to enact

---

[5] See the biography of Ibn Hesham based on the research by Mustapha al-Saqa and his two companions (second edition) 1375 AH or 1955 AD / Part two, pages 289-307.

laws concerning relationships between the genders in the Muslim society within and outside married life.

* * *

These are two examples of occasional sedition in the Muslim community during the Prophet's time. Islamic society faced another sedition, one with a purely political nature, after the death of the Prophet and it is the sedition of Saqifa.

This discord began when some of the senior companions of the Muhajireen and Ansar trespassed against the order of the Messenger of God that assigned the caliphate after the Prophet to Imam Ali ibn Abi Talib. The latter was the only individual with all of the talents and qualifications needed to lead the Islamic nation after the passing of the Prophet.

The conflict over the caliphate between the Muhajreen and Ansar was resolved in the Saqifa of Bani Sa'eda[6] in Imam Ali's absence and for the benefit of the tribe of Quraish. They gave allegiance to the first Caliph, Abu Bakr, after political maneuverings that used tribal logic, which almost led to a dangerous rift inside the newly born Islamic society.[7]

---

[6] The Saqifa of Bani Sa'eda was a place covered by palm tree fronds in the city of Yathreb. It a gathering place for the Ansar after the onset of Islam and their place for resolving issues and conducting negotiations.

[7] See by the same author: Neezam al-Hokom wa al-Idara fee al-Islam. Also see for the same author, Thawrat al-Hussein – Zouroufaha al-Ijtema'eyah wa Atharaha al-Insaneeyah, fifth edition, part 1.

Imam Ali's position was the biggest factor and the most far reaching in overcoming the conflict of Saqifa and its dangerous effects.

Imam Ali was a true man of Islamic legitimacy given his absolute and superior qualification among the best of the companions, his unique talents and the Prophet's direction that he was to succeed him as caliph.

Given his situation, he was fully within his rights to object and refuse the decision that was made outside of the proper bounds at the meeting in Saqifa, in pursuing his right to assume power. However, though he considered that to be his right he was facing a real sociopolitical challenge.

On the one hand, the Muslim society was in its infancy and was still vulnerable in terms of cohesion based on a common belief. The pre-Islamic values were still prevalent in the everyday life of the tribes that entered Islam about a year, or less, before the death of the Prophet. In the best of cases, these pre-Islamic values were just below the surface under a thin veneer of Islam. With the passing of enough time, these values would have withered and lost their effectiveness. In such a situation, any seemingly forceful political act would likely lead to dangerous rifts in the Muslim community and its cohesion and could also lead to a widespread reaction among the new Muslims.

On the other hand, there was a group of tribes that had already left Islam and some of them were following falsely declared prophets. The spread of the phenomenon of false prophets was a real threat to Islam and some of its leaders were forming a coalition that would unite their forces. They nearly controlled Yemen in the south and they controlled large areas of Hijaz and Najad in the north.

At first, Imam Ali turned to dissent and disapproval. He refused to acknowledge the results from the Saqifa meeting. He refused to leave his house. It became clear that his position of the decision of Saqifa would cause serious ramifications both in and outside of the city. However, the Imam quickly faced the political and social realities of the infant Muslim community and the potential dangers to Islam itself that could result from holding that position.

Had it not been that Imam Ali was the first man of the doctrine and the message, and the most aware and the one with the greatest sense of responsibility, he would not have paid any heed to the political and social realities of Islam. He would have persisted in his opposition until the end and taken advantage of the political and social realities for the sake of his pursuit of power.

However he already was the first man of the doctrine and the message and the absolute greatest Muslim with the sense of responsibility towards Islam. He was also the most vigilant about its prosperity, growth and deepening in the hearts and minds.

It is certain that ruling for him was not a personal pursuit but rather it was a means to an end, and it was bigger than individuals, generations or personal interests. It was broad and it was meant to last through the end of life as we know it, inclusive of the future generations in all centuries and all nations.

After the Prophet, Imam Ali was the father of Islam and he behaved as a caring father would. And so he was grandly patient with his personal wounds and deprivation for the sake of the largest cause in his life – the cause of Islam.

Without a doubt, all Muslims knew these facts about the Imam's personality and conscience. It would seem that his political rivals, when they undertook their successful adventure,[8] were counting on a number of assumptions including their belief that the Imam will put the best interests of Islam above his own.

The Imam pointed out the political consideration that prevented him from continuing with his opposition in a letter

---

[8] The indirect warning by the Caliph Omar bin al-Kahttab to Talha, Zubeir and others suggest a sense by everyone of the seriousness of the action they took and its large degree of venturing. He warned them about their opinions in relation to the way power was transitioned during the meeting at Saqifa (the pledge of allegiance to Abu Bakr was the least of it; May God protect from its evil).

to the people of Egypt sent with Malek al-Ashtar when the Imam appointed him its governor during his reign as caliph:

> ... I therefore withheld my hand until I saw that many people were reverting from Islam and trying to destroy the religion of Muhammad (may God bless him and his descendants). I then feared that if I did not protect Islam and its people and there occurred in it a breach or destruction, it would mean a greater blow to me than the loss of power over you which was, in any case, to last for a few days of which everything would pass away as the mirage passes away, or as the cloud scuds away. Therefore, in these happenings I rose until wrong was destroyed and disappeared, and religion attained peace and safety.[9]

The Imam's initial messianic position disappointed the hopes of many whose Islam was doubtful or who were faithful Muslims but saw the issue of governance from the perspective of tribal and familial interests due to their lack of maturity and consciousness.

Some people in both of these groups tried to change the Imam's initial messianic mind. However he rejected their attempts, stating that the situation was one of sedition and calling on them to assess the position in light of Islamic faith

---

[9] The Peak of Eloquence, Letters and Sayings, Letter number 62.

principles and to stay away from the pre-Islamic principles that seemed apparent through these attempts.

He declared this position on many occasions, including his speech to the people when Abu Sufian ibn Harb and al-Abbas ibn Abed Al-Muttalib called on him to accept their allegiance:

> *O People! Steer clear through the waves of mischief by boats of deliverance, turn away from the path of dissension and put off the crowns of pride. Prosperous is one who rises with wings (i.e. when he has power) or else he remains peaceful and others enjoy ease. It (i.e. the aspiration for Caliphate) is like turbid water or like a morsel that would suffocate the person who swallows it. One who plucks fruits before ripening is like one who cultivated in another's field.*[10]

* * *

Based on reports about Imam Ali in this regard, there are four characteristics for the occasional sedition.

1. A political crisis starts, possibly due to an insignificant event, generally unplanned and even occasional. However, oftentimes, other social forces, with secret agendas that are in conflict to the existing social system, interfere to benefit from these events and that political crisis in order to reach their own goals.

---

[10] The Peak of Eloquence, Sermon 5.

The political crisis could result from planned events with large impacts, such as the one in Saqifa. However, the groups that incite the events do not necessarily do so with the intent of opposing the prevailing order in society. Rather, they are bent on being in harmony with that system and seeking to strengthen it according to their beliefs and through their own authority.

2. In both of the above cases, the occasional strife revives some of the old values that had been abolished by the new system; due to weakness in oversight in the new system while its agents are occupied with the immediate political problems, or due to their leniency with some naïve political forces in order to earn their loyalty during the ongoing political conflict. However, in all cases, their old values do not return explicitly, rather they return disguised with new banners.

3. Often, the events that constitute the environment for sedition are raised by problems brought on by normal people or people with secondary importance on the social ladder. It affects such people as was the case in the dispute over water between Al-Ghafari (Jahjah) and Al-Juhani (Sinan). However, blood relations, friendships, interests and aspirations quickly politicize these events and take advantage of them. These events could be started because of problems raised by important people in the community or the events could

affect such people, such as was the case in the incidents of Ifk and Saqifa.

4. The legitimate and lawful power faces this sedition with calm and a heightened sense of responsibility. It avoids taking any action or emotional and retaliatory positions. This leads to serious consequences which make the situation more complex and strengthen the sedition. It also allows the hidden opposing forces, such as the hypocrites in the Islamic society, to take advantage of the emerging situation to achieve their own goals (see the first characteristic above).

Instead of facing the events of occasional sedition with violence and emotions, the leadership is careful to face it in a manner that gives priority to a solution for the benefit of principles and the general public and not for the benefit of individuals or families.

These, we believe, are the most prominent characteristics of occasional sedition.

DOMINANT SEDITION

This third kind of sedition, as we define it, is between broad sedition and the occasional one. Dominant sedition could rise due to significant political, legislative or faith-based deterioration in society at its beginning or after it reaches its peak.

It could also arise from an occasional sedition that the leadership neglected to face or ignored so it became a bigger issue in society. The state of deviation feeds on the deep contradictions in the depth of the social structure. It also feeds on the old values that were forced by the new system to withdraw from the social processes and into hiding.

The elite fails in resolving this issue because of their inability to do so or because of their inner rivalries and the bias of some towards deviation.

Time is also a factor that contributes to deviation. The longer deviation goes on unchecked or unaddressed, the stronger and more entrenched it becomes and the more widespread it is in the new areas it reached. It engulfs more people with convictions in its favor and further isolates and handicaps the elite.

Before long, this sedition, that implanted its claws in the core of society and that the elite failed to eliminate, becomes widespread and affects a lot of aspects of life. It becomes the norm, the law or practiced behavior, protected and safeguarded by convictions rooted in the culture. It becomes part of the structure of the culture and society.

We said that this happens before long from the start of sedition because deviation is usually easier and more convenient and makes life easier. That is how it tempts because it is more satisfying and more removed from liability and sacrifice.

However, deviation does not absorb or include all of the institutions in society, nor can it change all aspects of its cultural structure or accommodate all social classes within its concepts and new values, invented or revived. As such, it cannot completely destroy all progressive movement in society. It can hamper it but it cannot absolutely suspend, distort, or deform it. It does not reach the same degree as broad sedition but it is a dominant one.

With dominant sedition, the spirits of purity and authenticity remain in the community in general. They sustain its progressive movement in more than one facet of its life and its activities. And even though this spirit is frequently subject to setbacks for the society at large, it retains its full glow and effectiveness among small and limited groups, dispersed in the community and delivered from any deviation and steadfast on the straight path.

These authentic pure groups are the vanguard of the struggle against dominant sedition in society. They come between sedition and its ability to draw in all of society and become broad. It is through their perseverant and patient struggle that they prevent sedition from taking root and becoming established. They keep sedition unsettled and in a constant state of war.

Hence, communities in a state of broad sedition benefit from stability and consistency as a result of harmony between values, popular beliefs and general culture; all of which become integrated and support each other. As a result there is a state of equilibrium provided, which in turn delivers stability and consistency.

However, under dominant sedition, the situation is otherwise because there is little or big antagonism between institutions, values, beliefs and culture. This leads to a society in a constant state of anxiety, unrest and discord due to the presence of anti-sedition powers. These powers force those behind the sedition to move against them.

* * *

In the Islamic world, dominant sedition is one that took hold towards the later part of the caliphate of Othman ibn Affan. Imam Ali led the opposing movement to this sedition throughout the last years of his life. It continued after his martyrdom and became more violent and ferocious because motivation cooled and wills failed in effectively confronting it. And so it succeeded and became more prevalent before the era of revolutions and the apostasy movement.

Imam Ali spoke a great deal about sedition in all of its facets. We discuss its reasons, beginnings, means and reactions in the following.

HOW DOES SEDITION START?

How does sedition start? Imam Ali said:

The basis of the occurrence of evils are those desires which are acted upon and the orders that are innovated. They are against the Book of God. People co-operate with each other about them even though it is against the Religion of God. If wrong had been pure and unmixed it would not be hidden from those who are in search of it. And if right had been pure without admixture of wrong those who bear hatred towards it would have been silenced.

What is, however, done is that something is taken from here and something from there and the two are mixed! At this stage Satan overpowers his friends and they alone escape for whom virtue has been apportioned by God from before.[11]

This text reveals two factors that comprise dominant sedition.

Firstly, one's own measure of values defeating the use of objective measures, "...desires which are acted upon..." The leaders of this type of sedition use their own self-driven, emotional and self-serving impulses as a measure and the ultimate reference for values and behaviors instead of using the values of a doctrine or laws in society. It is through this approach that they take positions from events and people.

Secondly, the fall of the law and the violation of its sanctity on the practical level, "...the orders that are innovated. They are

---

[11] The Peak of Eloquence, Sermon 50.

against the Book of God." The personal factor overcomes the legal legitimacy through deception as those committing the sedition maintain the appearance of respecting the law and pretending to behave within its boundaries while at the same time, at the practical level, they are violating these laws every possible chance.

These two factors are the core of the dominant sedition: the fall of an objective measure of values from the moral and social and political relationships aspect, and the fall of the legal legitimacy from the perspective of public institutions, relationships, and the political, economic and social situations.

It is then possible that convictions allied with the dominant sedition form within new social groups: "...People cooperate with each other about them even though it is against the Religion of God." This reinforces the position of deviation in society and deepens its roots in the hearts and minds and broadens its coverage so that it includes new areas of life.

However, as we mentioned above, this does not reach the degree of full coverage in society. Justice and lawfulness continue having supporters and advocates in the community. They are, "...they alone escape for whom virtue has been apportioned by God from before." They are the ones who lead the fight against falsehood and sedition for the sake of the ultimate justice which is not to be confused with falsehood.

* * *

HOW DOES SEDITION START AND FUNCTION?

The Imam describes how sedition starts, functions and spreads in society in another sermon discussing dominant sedition and warning the Muslim community of it:

> ... *You, O people of Arabia, will be victims of calamities which have come near. You should avoid the intoxication of wealth, fear the disasters of chastisement, keep steadfast in the darkness and crookedness of mischief when its hidden nature discloses itself, its secrets become manifest and its axis and the pivot of its rotation gain strength. It begins in imperceptible stages but develops into great hideousness. Its youth is like the youth of an adolescent and its marks are like the marks of beating by stone. Oppressors inherit it by (mutual) agreement. The first of them serves as a leader for the latter one and the latter one follows the first one. They vie with each other in (the matter of) this lowly world, and leap over this stinking carcass. Shortly the follower will denounce his connection with the leader, and the leader with the follower. They will disunite on account of mutual hatred and curse one another when they meet.*[12]

---

[12] The Peak of Eloquence, Sermon 151.

In this text, the Imam outlined the mechanism for the movement of sedition, its growth and its spreading in society. The following highlight some of those characteristics:

1. The prevalence of opulence in society and the preoccupation of the elite with that opulence both lead to a community that loses its fighting messianic spirits. They are also keen on preserving its indulgent and trivial lifestyle as well as providing the appropriate means to reach even higher levels of indulgence and triviality.

   In this case, the elite is also afflicted with flabbiness, inability and cowardice. The prevalence of this spirit of opulence in a young society surrounded by opposing forces makes this society predisposed to the growth and spread of sedition. This is in addition to the internal weakness arising from groups within its ranks that lack a deep appreciation for its message – such was the case of the Muslim society at that time.

   Imam Ali warned of this by saying, "You should avoid the intoxication of wealth…"

2. In everyday life, there are occurrences or specific situations that cause confusion in how to deal with some of the messianic concepts or notions of belief in reality. For example, the changes that occurred as a result of the expansion of the conquests in Iran and the

Byzantine colonies... and the friction between the Iranian and the Eastern-Roman cultures... or the confusion that ensued after Othman bin Affan was killed. In these circumstances, the elite or the political leadership in the community might make impromptu decisions that are reactionary and lack prudence. One example is the reaction of some the companions to Imam Ali after Othman was assassinated. Immediately after receiving allegiance, Imam Ali demanded that those accused of killing Othman be arrested and punished. Some of the companions said to him, "Do you punish the people who helped against Othman?" Imam Ali answered them in a manner befitting of a prudent statesman with true insight into the ramifications of particular courses of action:

O my brothers! I am not ignorant of what you know, but how do I have the power for it while those who assaulted him are in the height of their power. They have superiority over us, not we over them. They are now in the position that even your slaves have risen with them and Bedouin Arabs too have joined them. They are now among you and are harming you as they like. Do you see any way to be able to do what you aim at? This demand is certainly that of the pre-Islamic (al-jahiliyyah) period and these people have support behind them.

When the matter is taken up, people will have different views about it. One group will think as you do, but another will not think as you think, and there will be still another group who will be neither this way nor that way. Be patient until people quieten down and hearts settle in their places so that rights can be achieved for people easily. Rest assured from me, and see what is given to you by me. Do not do anything which shatters your power, weakens your strength and engenders feebleness and disgrace. I shall control this affair as far as possible, but if I find it necessary the last treatment will, of course, be branding with a hot iron (through fighting).[13]

Thus, we see that Imam Ali asked those who were being hasty to instead be prudent and make wise decisions considering the context and time they were in. He urged them not to submit to the methods and reactions of the pre-Islamic era because that will lead to confusion and floundering in ideas and positions. In addition, errors in decision making will make the general environment more conducive for sedition. The Imam pointed that out by saying, "… keep steadfast in the darkness…"[14]

---

[13] The Peak of Eloquence, Sermon 168.

[14] The Peak of Eloquence, Sermon 151.

3. When the suitable environment is present as a result of the above-mentioned factors, sedition starts with simple and easy phenomena of deviation. This is received by society in general, and the political and ideological elite in particular, with tolerance and indifference and that is what allows these deviant phenomena a safe environment to grow and expand. The Imam expressed this by saying, "when its hidden nature discloses itself, its secrets become manifest."[15]

4. Unlike when sedition starts in an obscure manner, hiding behind excuses and disguising itself with treacherous messages, when sedition grows and expands it comes on strong with oppression and violence. It starts to deeply affect society with its characteristics. The Imam expressed this by saying, "Its youth is like the youth of an adolescent and its marks are like the marks of beating by stone."[16]

5. After sedition expands and includes more groups in society, it forms convictions and implants them more firmly in the mind of the public. These become a common and widespread culture that the authority uses to drive the sedition movement and direct the community according to its laws. The Imam expressed

---

[15] The Peak of Eloquence, Sermon 151.

[16] The Peak of Eloquence, Sermon 151.

this by saying, "Oppressors inherit it by (mutual) agreement. The first of them serves as a leader for the latter one and the latter one follows the first one."[17]

6. However, the political state of the leaders of sedition does not remain united and coherent after it has expanded and taken root in society. At that point, contradictions and personal traits for each group emerge as do the ambitions and fears for each group. This leads to division among the ranks of leadership, reducing them to bickering factions and drawing society into rivalries, arguments and civil war. The Imam expressed this by saying, "... Shortly the follower will denounce his connection with the leader, and the leader with the follower. They will disunite on account of mutual hatred and curse one another when they meet."[18]

* * *

The following text is where the Imam (a) tells his companions of what awaits them of sedition and woes after him, assigning them the responsibility for the rise and expansion of sedition along with all its consequent evils. They were passive in the face of the manifestations of sedition in their political environment and cultural infrastructure. Such passiveness

---

[17] The Peak of Eloquence, Sermon 151.

[18] The Peak of Eloquence, Sermon 151.

provided the necessary grounds and environment for the growth and proliferation of sedition, while they remained languid and shirked responsibility in supporting the cause and protecting their just legislative system:

> *O people! If you had not evaded support of the truth and had not felt weakness from crushing wrong then he who was not your match would not have aimed at you and he who overpowered you would not have overpowered you. But you roamed about the deserts (of disobedience) like Banu Isra'il (Children of Israel). I swear by my life that after me your tribulations will increase several times, because you will have abandoned the truth behind your backs, severed your connection with your near ones and established relations with remote ones...[19]*

WHAT IS A MUSLIM'S POSITION OF SEDITION WHEN IT STARTS?

As we have seen with sedition, truth is mixed with falsehood. What is right and wrong are confused and it becomes hard to tell the two apart.

In this case, the safest and most aligned position with the religious laws is to stay away from the sedition and refraining from participating altogether with either side. One cannot be sure that he is not committing a wrong when he thinks he is

---

[19] The Peak of Eloquence, Sermon 166.

the supporting the right, nor can one be sure that he is not fighting justice when he believes he is fighting the wrong.

The Imam advised of taking this position when sedition exists and the right and the wrong are mixed up. He said,

> *During civil disturbance be like an adolescent camel who has neither a back strong enough for riding nor udders for milking.*[20]

This is the proper position in the absence of a just Imam and when it is hard for a Muslim to discern right from wrong among the events before him. However, when there is a just Imam and he takes a position from the sedition, a Muslim needs to align his own position with that of the Imam's. At that point there would no longer be an excuse for inaction under the guise of fear of falling into the wrong. In this case, such a position would be one of cowardice and betrayal of the right. In fact, it could be even considered treason and support for the sedition from some perspectives because the unexcused inaction he may be providing an excuse for others to do the same.

During his tumultuous rule, the Imam faced such cowardly, traitorous and negative positions from some of the leaders in his community towards the sedition started by the opposing rebellious forces. He said addressing the people:

---

[20] The Peak of Eloquence, Letters and Sayings, Hadith number 1.

O people, throw away the reins of the horses who carry on their backs the weight of your hands (i.e. sins), do not cut away from your chief (Imam) otherwise you will blame yourself for your own doings. Do not jump in the fire which is in flames in front of you; keep away from its courses and leave the middle way for it. Because, by my life, the believer will die in its flames, and others will remain safe in it.

I am among you like a lamp in the darkness. Whoever enters by it will be lit from it...[21]

Here the Imam is forbidding his listeners from participating in the sedition; however, he does not prevent them from having a negative position from it. Instead, he instructs them to oppose it.

Participating in the sedition means conspiring with it. Taking a negative position does not mean leaving it unopposed. Both of these positions are wrong. Facing it, alongside the ruling and just Imam, is the proper position to take because the Imam provides guidance to what is right. He is the guide who does not mislead and he is the "lamp in the darkness" – shining light against the darkness of sedition and any other darkness.

In the beginning of Imam Ali's caliphate, some Muslims were confused regarding the sedition that had taken place. It rose

---

[21] The Peak of Eloquence, Sermon 187.

with the disobedience of Talha and Zubayr and the defiance by Muawiya as a result of the position of Abu Musa al-Ash'ari. The latter told the people of Kufa, when they called for the suppression of the rebellion by Talha and Zubayr, that such a situation is one of sedition and that the proper response to it was to refrain from participating.

The Imam clarified that such a position would be proper if the right and the wrong are mixed up; however, the situation is different when the right is made clear through the presence of a just Imam or through other means. In such a situation, inaction is treason.

Hence, the Imam labeled Talha and Zubayr's disobedience as sedition and he called on the people to confront and oppose them because the truth was made clear. As he marched on to Basra, he wrote to the people of Kufa:

> *...You should know that Medina has been vacated by its residents and they have abandoned it. It is boiling like a huge cooking pot and rebellion is fixed on its axis moving with full force. So, hasten towards your amir (commander) and proceed forward to fight your enemy...*[22]

---

[22] The Peak of Eloquence, Letters and Sayings, Letter number 1.

IMAM ALI'S POSITION FROM SEDITION DURING HIS TIME

What was the role of Imam Ali? And what was his position from the sedition that engulfed the Muslim community during his rule?

An examination of the political and ideological histories of Islam clearly reveals that Imam Ali was Islam's greatest savior from sedition. He saved the faith and its people from distortion and alteration brought forth by the sedition that savagely ravaged Muslims in the second half of Othman's caliphate.

Islam would have been disfigured, distorted and reduced had it not been for Imam Ali's leadership. Through his intellectual directives, political positions and military confrontations he countered sedition in all of its intellectual, political and military forms. Imam Ali's uncompromising stances revealed the sources of sedition and its advocates, giving all Muslims the ultimatum: supporting sedition or standing against it?

It did not matter that sedition subsequently garnered a large group of the people. It was important that it was exposed and through that exposure, Islam was safe from distortion and from the risk of fraud. Those who strayed had to find excuses for themselves.

The expectation and fear that sedition would emerge, along with sedition's associated activities and consequences, was a general obsession for Muslims. This was clearly shown by the extent of questions about sedition, the positions to take in its regard, and the Imam's frequent discussion about sedition, its dangers and circumstances.

Imam Ali was the only man to confront the sedition and rescue Islam from it. He did this with his high degree of spirituality, his strong and pure faith, his unmatched messianic spirit, his deep wisdom, his courage and his impeccable lifestyle.

The Prophet had informed him of this and he in turn understood his role by keeping watch on the movements of society over time.

There is a text of great importance that reveals to us Imam Ali's expected role in confronting sedition. It includes a prophetic vision for the future of the movement of history on one hand, and a prophetic vision for Imam Ali's role in this movement.

Sharif Al-Radi cited this text as did Ibn Abi Al-Hadid in his explanation (9/205-207) of the account by al-Sharif and of another more simple account. It would seem that the other account was more of a statement by the Imam, whereas Al-Radi's account was a sermon in answer to a question he was asked. A man had come up to him during a sermon and said to him, "O Commander of the Faithful, tell us about this disturbance and whether you enquired about it from the Holy Prophet." The Imam replied:

When God, the Glorified sent down the verse:

'Alif lam mim. What! Do people imagine that they will be let off on (their) saying: "We believe!" and they will not be tried?' (Qur'an, 29:1-2)

I came to know that the disturbance would not befall us so long as the Prophet (peace and blessing of God be upon him and his progeny) is among us.

So I said, 'O Prophet of God, what is this disturbance of which God, the Sublime, has informed you?' He replied, 'O Ali, my people will create trouble after me.' I said, 'O Prophet of God, on the day of Uhud, when people had fallen martyrs and I was not among them, and that was distressing for me, did you not say to me, cheer up, as martyrdom is for you hereafter?' The Prophet replied, 'Yes it is so, but what about your enduring at present?' I said, 'O Prophet of God, this is not an occasion for endurance, but rather an occasion for cheering up and gratefulness.'

Then he said: 'O Ali, people will fall into mischief through their wealth, will show obligation to God on account of their faith, will expect His mercy, will feel safe from His anger and regard His unlawful matters as lawful by raising false doubts and by their misguiding desires. They will then hold lawful (the use of) wine by calling it barley water, a bribe by calling it a gift, and taking of usurious interest by calling it sale.' I said, 'O Prophet of God, how should I deal with them at the time, whether to hold them to have gone back in heresy or just in revolt.' He said, 'In revolt.'[23]

The Imam was watchful to face sedition and expose it. After the Prophet, the Imam was Islam's guardian protecting it from fraud and distortion. He was able to protect the faith and maintain its true form through his stands in belief, ideology, laws and work. He clearly rendered sedition a crisis within Islam and prevented the sedition from penetrating the faith.

The Imam expressed on more than one occasion his unique role in history. He was the only leader who was able to confront and expose sedition. Among his sayings,

> *... I have put out the eye of revolt. No one except me advanced towards it when its gloom was swelling and its madness was intense...*[24]

* * *

There were many seditions in Islam. The most dangerous and destructive of those seditions was by the Umayyads, which ravaged society during the second half of Othman's reign with its evil winds. It became greater after his death. Most of Imam Ali's efforts in the last years his life were occupied with confronting this revolt intellectually, politically and militarily.

---

[23] The Peak of Eloquence, Sermon 156.
[24] The Peak of Eloquence, Sermon 93.

Imam Ali (a) seized every opportunity to talk to his community about this sedition showing them its current and future dangers. He did this to make them psychologically strong against it, mentally aware of its dangers, determined to work on confronting and suppressing it, and resolute in refusing it even if it succeeded.

He said:

> When mischiefs come they confuse (right with wrong) and when they clear away they leave a warning. They cannot be known at the time of approach but are recognized at the time of return. They blow like the blowing of winds, striking some cities and missing others.
>
> Beware that the worst mischief for you in my view is the mischief of Banu Umayyah, because it is blind and also creates darkness. Its sway is general but its ill effects are for particular people. He who remains clear-sighted in it would be affected by distress, and he who remains blind in it would avoid the distress.[25]

Its tribulation was broad because its advocates were the rulers themselves. Thus, its political and ideological evils affected the entire community. This mischief affected particular people because its heaviest strikes were directed at the faithful and aware elite. They had remained intact from the disease of

---

[25] The Peak of Eloquence, Sermon 93.

mischief and put themselves in a position to fight the dominant sedition.

The responsibility in this sedition lies with those who are aware of it. They know it, they know the truth and they cower from confrontation or collude with it against justice. And those who are blind to it and were ignorant of its implications and dangers are excused because of their ignorance.

THE TRIUMPH OF
APOSTASY

Apostasy here does not mean religious apostasy from Islam. We have previously seen the Prophet's guidance to Ali when he asked the Messenger of God, "How do I categorize them then? In the category of apostasy or that of sedition?" The Prophet said, "Sedition."

Here we mean the political and ideological apostasy. When sedition prevailed politically after the martyrdom of Imam Ali, it started to entrench itself by imposing its ideological and social values in the general culture. It also imprinted its own character on relationships in the community.

* * *

Through his great insight, the Imam saw that strife will prevail. His insight into this was one of causes for his deep pain. He also saw that sedition could only be resisted with great effort and struggle. Tolerating and giving it respite would only allow it an opportunity to prevail.

It pained him that his society, for various reasons, chose to face sedition in silence, or in other words, chose not to face the coming sedition at all. He would compare between the Prophet's companions and his own and he would remind them that the cultural orientation and the leadership are the same. Still, he realized that the degree of loyalty differed:

> *... By God, whatever the Prophet told them, I am here telling you the same and whatever you hear today is not different from what they heard yesterday. The eyes that were opened for them and the hearts that were made for them at that time, just the same have been given to you at this time.*
>
> *By God, you have not been told anything that they did not know and you have not been given anything which they were deprived. Certainly you have been afflicted by a calamity (which is like a she-camel) whose nose-string is moving about and whose strap is loose o in whatever condition these deceitful people are should not deceive you, because it is just a long shadow whose term is fixed.*[1]

On several occasions, he repeated the comparison between the Prophet's companions and his own. He saw that his

---

[1] The Peak of Eloquence, Sermon 89.

companions' way of confronting sedition foreshadowed its victory after him. He shared this view in many occasions with his community, including:

> *...By God in Whose power my life lies, these people (Mu`awiyah and his men) will overcome you not because they have a better right than you but because of their hastening towards the wrong with their leader and your slowness about my right (to be followed). People are afraid of the oppression of their rulers while I fear the oppression of my subjects. I called you for war but you did not come. I warned you but you did not listen. I called you secretly as well as openly, but you did not respond. I gave you sincere counsel, but you did not accept it.[2]*

This text, like many others of the same nature, reveals that Imam Ali's estimation and analysis of the victory of sedition was not a result of imprudence. Rather, it arose as a result of the existence of the objective reasons in the political and social arenas whose actions were interacting in the political community opposing sedition.

This community lost its impact and relinquished its spirit of resistance in confronting sedition. It was practically separated from its leadership and wallowed in negativity. It chose the

---

[2] The Peak of Eloquence, Sermon 97.

easy life, void of obligations towards the message and the struggle. The Imam said:

> *Then after this there will appear another arouser of mischief who will destroy ruined things. The heart will become wavering after being normal, men will be misled after safety, desires will multiply and become diversified and views will become confused. Whoever proceeds towards this mischief will be ruined and whoever strives for it will be annihilated. They will be biting each other during it as the wild asses bite each other in the herd. The coils of the rope will be disturbed and the face of affairs will be blinded. During it sagacity will be on the ebb, and the oppressors will (get the opportunity to) speak. This mischief will smash the Bedouins with its hammers and crush them with its chest... You should not become landmarks of mischiefs and signs of innovations but should adhere to that on which the rope of the community has been wound and on which the pillars of obedience have been founded.[3]*

The Imam illustrates some of the attributes of the victory of sedition:

1. Sedition takes over other areas of the community, "men will be misled after safety," and deviant thoughts

---

[3] The Peak of Eloquence, Sermon 151.

become more deeply rooted, "the heart will become wavering after being normal."

2. Society becomes at a loss as a result of an unexpected victory that imposes new unfamiliar concepts.

3. At its heights, sedition destroys anyone who stands up to it.

The Imam depicts other manifestations for that victory in another one of his sermons:

> ... Nevertheless, now the wrong has set itself on its places and ignorance has ridden on its riding beasts. Unruliness has increased while the call for virtue is suppressed. Time has pounced upon like a devouring carnivore, and wrong is shouting like a camel after remaining silent. People have become brothers over ill doings, have forsaken religion, and are united in speaking lie but bear mutual hatred in the matter of truth. When such is the case, the son would be a source of anger (instead of coolness of the eye to parents) and rain the cause of heat, the wicked would abound and the virtuous would diminish. The people of this time would be wolves, its ruler's beasts, the middle class men gluttons and the poor (almost) dead. Truth would go down, falsehood would overflow, affection would be claimed with tongues but people would be quarrelsome at heart. Adultery would be the key to

lineage while chastity would be rare and Islam would be worn overturned like the skin.[4]

In this sermon, the Imam details the characteristics of sedition when it prevails and overtakes society. It controls its institutions, deepens its roots therein and forces its beliefs and values on that society.

These characteristics can be summarized as follows:

1. The deeply rooted spirit of tyranny among the rulers, a tendency towards oppression and tyranny against the ruled, and the decline of the messianic message in the governing institutions

2. The corruption of human relationships within the community, a decline in morals, and the prevalence of self-interests among the people. The Imam's saying related to this is very eloquent. He says, "… affection would be claimed with tongues but people would be quarrelsome at heart."

3. Decadence in the family institution and sexual deviance.

This is all summarized with the Imam's saying, "… and Islam would be worn overturned like the skin." Another similar saying by the Imam:

---

[4] The Peak of Eloquence, Sermon 108.

"O people! A time will come to you when Islam would be capsized as a pot is capsized with all its contents."[5]

---

[5] The Peak of Eloquence, Sermon 103.

SUFFERING

When sedition wins its victory brings unjust rule. The nation is then only seen as an opportunity or platform for authoritarian rule and a source of monetary gain.

It adopts unethical rule because its leaders follow their rash motivations in public policy, instead of logic, law and justice. Invariably, this leads to many victims. Among those victims are the previous political opponents who in the end were defeated. Also among its victims are its allies when it was weak who were no longer needed when it became stronger. Those who are heedless of its evils and dangers, along with those who were neutral during the fight between sedition and the forces of good also fall victim. They were surprised when it prevailed and so they objected or feigned opposition to it. The greatest victim is the nation as a whole. Sedition transforms the nation to a source of oppression, wealth, opulence and entertainment for the elite, and uses it as a means for suppression by its allies.

Thus begins the suffering a nation from sedition, from its injustice and domination, from its enmity which spreads like an epidemic and affects every group in a defeated society with different means of aggression: moral, political, and economic.

The Imam provided vivid and expressive imagery of the suffering of the nation after the victory of sedition. Among his sayings:

> *... By God, you will find Banu Umayyah after me worst people for yourselves, like the old unruly she-camel who bites with its mouth, beats with its fore-legs, kicks with its hind legs and refuses to be milked. They would remain over you until they would leave among you only those who benefit them or those who do not harm them.*
> *Their calamity would continue until your seeking help from them would become like the seeking of help by the slave from his master or of the follower from the leader. Their mischief would come to you like evil eyed fear and pre-Islamic fragments, wherein there would be neither minaret of guidance nor any sign (of salvation) to be seen.[1]*

Thus, the people suffer in different ways from sedition after its victory:

---

[1] The Peak of Eloquence, Sermon 93.

1. Tyrannical rule that eliminates all those opposed to its opinion and doctrine through violence and cruelty.

2. Humiliation that destroys human dignity, distorts the spirit, and renders a slave he who does not dare raise his voice and express his opinion. Rather, he submits to inevitable blind obedience, not emanating from conviction but imposed by fear of punishment.

* * *

Imam Ali said:

By God, they would continue like this until there would be left no unlawful act before God but they would make it lawful and no pledge but they would break it, and until there would remain no house of bricks or of woollen tents but their oppression would enter it. Their bad dealings would make them wretched, until two groups of crying complainants would rise, one would cry for his religion and the other for this world and the help of one of you to one of them would be like the help of a slave to his master, namely when he is present he obeys him, but when the master is away he backbites him. The highest among you in distress would be he who bear best belief about God. If God grants you safety accept it, and if you are put in trouble endure it, because surely '...(good) result is for the God-fearing' (7:128)[2]

---

[2] The Peak of Eloquence, Sermon 98.

In this sermon, the Imam depicts other forms of suffering and torment:

1. The disregard of the sanctity of law by the ruling class – it is supposed to protect the laws in terms of application while ruling in the name of the religion.

2. The expansion of injustice so it affects all classes in the nation, the city dwellers and the Bedouins.

3. The humiliation and devastation to the dignity of humans, which, as a result of all of suffering, becomes more similar to the dignity of a slave.

This reality makes suffering more encompassing in matters of religion and life. The most aware and the strongest in the face of the temptations of sedition and its terror are the ones who suffer the most.

However, the Imam advised this enlightened group, who were not consumed by sedition, to be patient because sedition could not be resisted at that stage. All resistance efforts, while sedition is at the height of its victories, are wasted and lead the legitimate side to further weakening, isolation, and vulnerability.

* * *

The Imam said in relation to the above:

I notice that misguidance has stood on its center and spread (all round) through its off-shoots. It weighs you

with its weights and confuses you with its measures. Its
leader is an out-cast from the community. He persists on
misguidance. So on that day none from among you would
remain except as the sediment in a cooking pot or the dust
left after dusting a bundle. It would scrape you as leather
is scraped, and trample you as harvest is trampled, and
pick out the believer as a bird picks out a big grain from
the thin grain.[3]

In this text, the Imam continues to uncover the facets of suffering. The rule of tyranny neglects the application of the law because it leads under a lost banner. This rule behaves based on instinct alone and as such, it tramples the nation and erodes its strength and pride rendering it into a weak entity with no free will. It becomes like leather that has been scrapped so much that it loses all of its toughness and like the harvest that has been trampled so much that it crumbles.

Despite all of this, sedition is unable to prevail over absolutely. The elite of the elite preserve themselves despite financial corruption, moral oppression, and cultural distortion. Their numbers may be small but they are authentic, pure, and impervious to tyranny, distortion, temptation or terror.

* * *

On a related matter the Imam said:

---

[3] The Peak of Eloquence, Sermon 108.

During it sagacity will be on the ebb, and the oppressors will (get the opportunity to) speak. This mischief will smash the Bedouins with its hammers and crush them with its chest.

In its dust the single marchers will be lost, and in its way the horsemen will be destroyed. It will approach with the bitterness of destiny and will give pure blood (instead of milk). It will breach the minarets of faith and shatter the ties of firm belief. The wise will run away from it while the wicked will foster it. It will thunder and flash (like lightning). It will create a severe disaster. In it kinship will be forsaken and Islam will be abandoned. He who declaims it will also be affected by it, and he who flees from it will (be forced to) stay in it. Among them some will be unavenged martyrs and some will be stricken with fear and seek protection. They will be deceived by pledges...[4]

In this chapter, and some of the text in this chapter, the Imam highlights how injustice impacts the Bedouins. This signals the ultimate impact of injustice and oppression based on the social structure and cultural situation of society at that time. The Bedouins are removed from the reach of the government and its mechanisms because of their way of life. As such, they enjoy better chances than the city dwellers to escape the evils of

---

[4] The Peak of Eloquence, Sermon 151.

political oppression. However, a victorious sedition is so strong and so violent that even the Bedouins are not safe from it or its evils.

The Imam also highlighted other forms of struggling in this sermon; the humiliation, the approach of oppression, transcending laws, and decadence in human relations.

* * *

The Imam said:

> *At that time there will remain no house or tent but oppressors would inflict it with grief and inject sickness in it. On that day no one in the sky will listen to their excuse and no one on the earth will come to their help. You selected for the governance (caliphate) one who is not fit for it, and you raised him to a position which was not meant for him. Shortly God will take revenge from every one who has oppressed, food for food and drink for drink, namely (they will be given) colocynth for eating, myrrh and aloes for drinking, and fear for an inner and the sword for an outer covering. They are nothing but carrier-beasts laden with sins and camels laden with evil deeds.[5]*

In this excerpt the Imam shows the comprehensive nature of this sedition. The Imam reminded the populace in every era of

---

[5] The Peak of Eloquence, Sermon 158.

the objective cause that created it – the sedition – and allowed it to be. That cause is the lack of legitimacy in the ruler and the regime, with the pursuit of special interests, individual and tribal greed, and neglecting the responsibilities involved in the fight against falsehood and its people.

* * *

The Imam goes on to address the Kharajites, telling them of their fate in the coming regime where they will find no justice, equity, understanding their circumstances, or the aspirations they have, which they found in the system of justice that the Imam himself led:

> *Beware! Certainly you will meet, after me, overwhelming disgrace and a sharp sword and tradition that will be adopted by the oppressors as a norm towards you.*

* * *

Sedition becomes victorious and its authority becomes grand. Its conceptions reign and its values are forced on society. That carries on for years. The mutiny that reigns only gets stronger, spreading into every corner of society, and generation after generation adopts this way of thinking taking it as norm and custom.

This belief is wrong. The course of history does not stop at any specific point. It continues in its path of change and transformation. Sedition may be able to achieve a victory and solidify its political authority. But this will not be final outcome of sedition's development. Sedition will continue to face renewed resistance.

This resistance arises out of a truth that recuperated some of its strength. It does not bear to remain silent. It expresses itself through revolution. Yet the aim of the revolution is not military victory – that may be farfetched in that period of history – but to break the clout of sedition. It hampers a portion of sedition's destructive work in the faith and character of the nation. It deprives sedition of its stability and security. It forces sedition into a defensive position where destructive policies must be abandoned. It forces sedition to return – even for a short period – toward reason.

This resistance may also arise out of sedition itself. It generates new seditions that become a nuisance to the old guard. It replaces the old government with a new one. In that transition period, there would be a period of relief for the people of faith – a respite for the supporters of truth due to the inattentiveness of the political authority.

Imam Ali said,

> *Until people begin thinking that the world is attached to the Umayyads, would be showering its benefits on them, and lead them to its clear spring for watering, and that their whip and sword will not be removed from the*

people. Whoever thinks so is wrong. There are rather a few drops from the joys of life, which they would suck for a while and then vomit out the whole of it.[6]

In another excerpt he said in an address to the Umayyads,

This world did not appear sweet to you in its pleasures and you did not secure milk from its udders except after having met it when its nose-rein was trailing and its leather girth was loose. For certain people its unlawful items were like [bent branches laden with fruit] while its lawful items were far away and unavailable. By God, you would find it like a long shade up to a fixed time.

The earth is vacant [of any opposition to you]. Your hands in it are extended while the hands of the leaders are held away from you. Your swords are hanging over them while their swords are held away from you.

Surely, for every blood [that is shed] there is an avenger and for every right there is a claimant. The avenger for our blood is like the judge [judging on] his own claim. It is God – who is not stumped by any petitioner and is not evaded by any fugitive. I swear by Allah, O' Umayyad clan, shortly you will see it [i.e. your possession] in the hands of others and in the house of your enemy.[7]

He also said,

---

[6] The Peak of Eloquence, Sermon 87.

[7] The Peak of Eloquence, Sermon 105.

I swear and again swear that the Umayyad clan will spit it out [i.e. political authority] as phlegm is spat and thereafter they will never taste it nor relish its flavor so long as day and night rotate.[8]

* * *

This is how the Imam sees with his foresight that illuminates the horizons of a future that is enveloped in darkness. He sees history's course of excess and the political powers that are brewing within society and will be born in the future. They would deprive sedition of the pleasures of its victories and push it into a defensive position. The governing authorities are replaced with new forces – forces that may either be just or unjust.

---

[8] The Peak of Eloquence, Sermon 158.

REVOLUTION

Sedition grows. Its grasp becomes overpowering. Yet its enemies begin to grow little by little. They would be of its children, which suffered because of it. They would be the vanguard that the sedition was founded to oppose. They would be those who did not oppose the sedition at the outset, but after its victory, they had become amongst its victims.

It is all of these groups who the Commander of the Faithful points to when he describes the suffering wrought by sedition when he said, "...until two groups of crying complainants would rise, one would cry for his religion and the other for this world..."[1]

All of these individuals would see that the regime – the one established by sedition – is oppressive. Each group would see oppression from its unique point of view.

---

[1] The Peak of Eloquence, Sermon 98.

Some would see the oppression of the regime from the perspective of their personal, factional, or tribal interests. They would not care if the revolution usurped the rights of other individuals or groups. They would not care about the regime's illegitimacy and that it has obstructed the nation's missionary role in the world. And that it had transformed the nation into a composite of warring factions that has lost its sense of unity.

Others would see the oppression of the regime through a religious and missionary lens. They would transcend personal, factional, and tribal interests.

All of these factions that become infuriated with the regime would see its oppression; oppression that is wrought by the contradiction of law – as seen by each faction from its distinct perspective – and the policies of the state.

Each faction, with its distinct set of tools, would prepare for work. The goal would be to correct the status quo by eliminating the divergence between the state's political realities and the law. This would either be through compulsion of the ruling faction to base its policies on law, or by changing the ruling faction altogether.

The means to achieve this corrective process is revolution.

Thus, violent demonstration against the seditious regime and its policies may be in the form of a just revolution, or it may be a quandary within the larger seditious movement. By the latter, we mean the emergence of a new sedition born out of the failure of the ruling seditious regime to please political forces within society that champion the same goals and ideology.[2]

Violent demonstration against the realities of the seditious regime has a great and significant benefit, regardless of whether those who implement such demonstration are just or seditious. It instills turmoil and anxiety into the regime and inhibits it from enjoying any sense of stability and security – stability and security which it would use to distort the faith and corrupt morals.

It allows for the perseverant forces of good within the nation to breathe a little. It allows them to play their role in raising awareness throughout the nation with a relative freedom that they would not have enjoyed had the seditious regime enjoyed peace and stability.

* * *

The Imam had a positive outlook to the demonstrative movements against the seditious regime that would come after him. If it wasn't feasible – in light of the implications of history's trajectory – for complete legitimacy to prevail in the short term, it would still be positive for the seditious regime

---

[2] We use the term *thawra* (revolution) – in the context of Islamic history – to refer to a political action that enjoys legitimacy. Anything else is alternatively called a *tamarrud* (rebellion), *khuruj* (insurrection), or *fitna* (sedition). Still, we named this section 'revolution' even though it will encompass a study of all forms of violent demonstration (whether legitimate or not) simply for rhetorical reasons – favoring a simple heading over a more convoluted one.

not to have the opportunity to solidify and take root. It would still be positive for the seditious regime to remain in a state of fear and caution, always on the defensive.

This is the reason behind his proclamation about the Kharijites, who manifested sedition through complete rejection of any governmental system. Thus, they were apt to become a potent nuisance for the triumphant seditious regime.

The Imam had disallowed armed conflict with the Kharijites after his passing. When he fought and defeated them at the Battle of Nahrawan – after they had refused all gestures of peace from him – they had been a destructive force against a just government. But once the seditious regime emerged triumphant, they became a distractive and paralyzing nuisance to the tyrannical and deviant government. It would hinder the regime from continuing its political and financial tyranny and implementing its plans for distortion of faith and its rituals.

Imam Ali had said,

> *Do not fight the Kharijites after me, because one who seeks right but does not find it, is not like one who seeks wrong and finds it.*[3]

He saw revolution coming.

---

[3] The Peak of Eloquence, Sermon 61.

He does not describe whether this revolution is just and upright, or oppressive and seditious. He only foreshadows the triumphant seditious regime would not enjoy victory and stability for long. Rather, it would soon be wrested of the delight of victory and the liberty of triumph and political and social stability. Bloody revolts will ensue one after the other until finally defeating the sedition of the Umayyad clan and ending their reign.

He said to an audience, speaking of sedition and its victory, and the impeding suffering it would beget,

> *Thereafter, God would dispel it from you like the removal of the skin [from flesh] through one who would humiliate them, drag them by necks, and make them drink full cups [i.e. he would not show any mercy]. He would not extend them anything but the sword and not clothe them save with fear. At that time Quraysh would wish at the cost of the world and all its contents to find me standing once more – even if it were only for the duration of the slaughter of a camel – in order that I may accept from them [the whole of] that of which at present I am asking them only a part but they are not giving me.[4]*

The Imam saw that one of the biggest objectives of the seditious regime was to dismantle the political and religious

---

[4] The Peak of Eloquence, Sermon 93.

forces standing in opposition to it. It did not matter whether or which of those opposing factions retained their pure Islamic values or were corrupted by sedition in one way or another.

Yet he also saw that the attempts of the seditious regime to dismantle these opposition factions will not continue with success. The trajectory of history would reunite these forces on the basis of a new political framework. Those would result in an end for any stability surrounding the seditious Umayyad regime.

Imam Ali said,

> *By God, even if they disperse you under every star, God would surely collect you on a day that would be most horrid for them.*[5]

He also said,

> *They will divide after their unity and scatter away from their origin. Some of them will stick to the branches, bending down as the branches bend. This until God, the Sublime, will collect them together for a day that will be most horrid for the Umayyad clan, just as the scattered bits of clouds collect together in the autumn. God will create affection among them [i.e. among the factions opposing the Umayyad regime]. Then He will make them into a strong mass like the mass of clouds. He will then*

---

[5] The Peak of Eloquence, Sermon 106.

open doors for them to flow out from their provenance like the flood of the two gardens [of Sheba] – from which neither valleys nor highlands remained safe, and whose flow could be repulsed neither by strong mountains nor by high lands. God will scatter them in the midst of His valleys and then make them flow like streams throughout the earth. Through them He will arrange the taking of rights of one people by another people and make one people to stay in the houses of another people. By God, all what they would hold from after position and esteem will dissolve as fat dissolves on the fire.[6]

* * *

One of his greatest visions into the course of history was his foreshadowing of the Kharijites' insurrection, and how it will grow and branch out, despite its apparent defeat and collapse. When the Kharijites were defeated, some said to him "O Commander of the Faithful, the entire faction was killed!" He replied,

By God! No, not yet. They still exist in the loins of men and wombs of women. Whenever a chief would appear from among them, he would be cut down until the last of them would turn thieves and robbers.[7]

---

[6] The Peak of Eloquence, Sermon 166.

[7] The Peak of Eloquence, Sermon 60.

This is how revolution comes in the aftermath of sedition's triumph, not allowing it to take delight in stability. Revolution disables sedition's tools and prevents it from spreading its ideology in the nation. By this, it creates a chance for the remaining forces of good to enjoy a bit of security, thereby allowing it some degree of freedom by which it can keep the torch of purity lit in the darkness of sedition. Many hearts and minds will look towards the colossal hope of a grand and final victory.

HOPE

The individual lives in the present, but is being tugged by both ends – the past and the future. Mankind does not forget. The individual carries the past in his conscience, memory, and makeup of his presence. He is burdened by his sorrows and delights, fears and hopes. He carries them towards the future. His path is lit by the rays of hope, which fill his heart with aspirations for a better life. Yet, his hopes are tortured by confusion, anxiety, and fear of disappointment.

This reality is evident in the lives of individuals, and it is no less significant in the lives of nations, societies, and groups.

Islam, in its religious teachings, stood against excessive hopes. When hope dominates the temperament of an individual, it makes him unrealistic. It traps him within his own imagination. It ferments a sense of selfishness in a way that makes him unconcerned for others. This is definitively rejected in a religion that places care for others a foundational tenant of upright human character.

Excessive hopes also stand in the way of many opportunities for moral and spiritual excellence. Quranic texts in this regard are many, and so are the texts of prophetic traditions. The teachings of Imam Ali in *the Peak of Eloquence* are also constant in warning against getting lost in hope.[1]

Naturally, this does not mean that moderate and realistic hopes are immoral from an Islamic perspective. How would this be the case when God the Almighty clearly warns of and forbids despondency in the Holy Quran? The Quran's verses remind us of God's mercy and clemency. We see this in Jacob's teachings to his sons when he sent them to look for Joseph and his brother,

> *Go, my sons, and look for Joseph and his brother, and do not despair of Allah's mercy. Indeed no one despairs of Allah's mercy except the faithless lot.*[2]

Jacob applied the principle of legitimate hope in a specific circumstance – the circumstance of his personal tragedy and his family.

Thus, hope in reality is a fundamental truth of humanity. Loss of hope is a psychological ailment and not a healthy symptom. This is on the individual level.

---

[1] For a more detailed and in-depth study on this, see the chapter on 'Good Counsel' in our book *Studies in The Peak of Eloquence*.

[2] The Holy Quran, 12:87.

As for the collective level of nations, societies, and groups, hope is a greatly significant and foundational factor. It energizes the movement of history and accelerates it. It allows it to easily triumph against any obstacle or hardship.

Objective hope is based in realistic considerations founded on human effort, along with doctrinal and spiritual considerations. It occupies a significant and foundational part of divine teachings for humanity as it walks in the path of faith.

The Quran consists of a number of definitive verses that give God's promise of triumph and honor for the people of faith and their leaders – the prophets and their righteous disciples.

God the Almighty said,

> *Indeed We shall help Our apostles and those who have faith in the life of the world and on the day when the witnesses rise up.*[3]

God Almighty also said,

> *Certainly We wrote in the Psalms, after the Torah: 'Indeed My righteous servants shall inherit the earth.'*[4]

In another verse, He said,

---

[3] The Holy Quran, 40:51.
[4] The Holy Quran, 21:105.

The earth indeed belongs to God, and He gives its inheritance to whomever He wishes of His servants, and the outcome will be in favor of the God-wary.[5]

God Almighty gave the directive to his Messenger Muhammad (s) and the Muslims that hope in triumph and a better life must remain alive and well – a motivation for exertion even in the most dire moments of disappointment, defeat, and lack of support. The hopes of triumph would be realized in the end in the most amazing fashion, just as despondency enters the heart of the believers and the honorable messengers reach the edge of despair.

We did not send [any apostles] before you except as men from among the people of the towns, to whom We revealed. Have they not travelled over the land so that they may observe how was the fate of those who were before them? And the abode of the Hereafter is surely better for those who are God-wary. Do you not exercise your reason? When the apostles had almost lost hope and thought that they had been told lies, Our help came to them, and We delivered whomever We wished, and Our punishment will not be averted from the guilty lot. There is certainly a moral in their accounts for those who possess intellect. This [Quran] is not a fabricated discourse; rather, it is a confirmation of what was [revealed] before

---

[5] The Holy Quran, 7:128.

it, and an elaboration of all things, and a guidance and mercy for a people who have faith.[6]

* * *

Collective hope for a brighter and less agonizing future – one that is full of happiness and free of anguish – is based on a divine promise. It is, therefore, not an adventurous dream of the future. Rather, it is a visionary march toward the future.

It is a hope that rejects the realities of experience filled with obstacles in favor of an ideal future conditioned on exertion with sincerity for the sake of God. For the sake of God, it builds life, constructs the Earth, and reforms societies. This future is also conditioned on perseverance over persecution at the side of God. It is conditioned on honesty in dealing with life and society. It is conditioned on satisfaction with God Almighty's judgment.

The prophetic tradition is full of narrations that plant the seeds of hope in the hearts of mankind. It fills their awareness of glad tidings of a better future based on the divine promise.

* * *

Deep reflection on the text of the Holy Book and the prophetic tradition that elucidate the relationship between God and mankind – as well as reflection on the law derived from these

---

[6] The Holy Quran, 12:109-11.

two sources – will allow us to see the nature of the relationship. This relationship is built on three factors that are the foundation of human society, its continuity, growth, and development.

First is the boundless and unconditional blessings on the level of material life that allows for continuity and growth toward betterment. God created mankind and imbued him with intellectual, personal, and spiritual skills that allow him to interact with an environment set at his disposal. These skills allow mankind to discover the treasures and resources of creation, learn its laws, and employ these discoveries to enhance the life of the individual and the species.

Second is the mercy that God has made 'incumbent upon Himself'[7] and which 'encompasses all things.'[8] He is clement towards shortcomings – whether on an individual or a collective level – and forbearing over sins and mistakes. He grants recurring opportunities for corrective action, mending

---

[7] God Almighty says, "Say: To whom belongs whatever is in the heavens and the earth?' Say: To God. He has made mercy incumbent upon Himself...." (The Holy Quran, 6:12). He also says, "When those who have faith in Our signs come to you, say: Peace to you! Your Lord has made mercy incumbent upon Himself. Whoever of you commits an evil [deed] out of ignorance and then repents after that and reforms, then He is indeed all-forgiving, all-merciful." (The Holy Quran, 6:54)

[8] God Almighty says, "Your Lord is dispenser of an all-embracing mercy, but His punishment will not be averted from the guilty lot." (The Holy Quran, 6:147) He also says, "I visit My punishment on whomever I wish, but My mercy embraces all things. Soon I shall appoint it for those who are God-wary and give the zakat and those who believe in Our signs." (The Holy Quran, 7:156)

deviance, atonement, and repentance to God Almighty, and to act in accordance with his laws once more.

This reality stems from the equation of two universal realities – God's infinite and all-encompassing good, and the objective truth embedded in Islamic thought that mankind was created weak.[9]

The exceptions to this reality, which bring pain and suffering, are of two types.

First, there are some that arise out of the nature and its laws – laws that are set for the grand purpose of the advancement of mankind regardless of time or geographic location. This makes the laws of nature just, even though it may inflict some suffering on a group of individuals in a certain space or time. This is the case with natural disasters that occur without the interference or shortcoming on the part of mankind.

There are also disasters that occur due to mankind's actions or inactions or due to their non-adherence to the law. In our modern times, this includes phenomena such as pollution, or the extortion and exploitation of third world countries at the hand of industrialized nations. These types of disasters are of the second type – ones that occur due to human choice such as impatience in pursuit of prosperity when the time is not yet ripe or due to transgression of groups over others.

---

[9] God Almighty said, "God desires to lighten your burden, for man was created weak." (The Holy Quran, 4:28).

Third is the glad tiding from God Almighty that the matters of life and society will become better and better. However, this glad tiding will not occur by a pure miracle. The fulfillment of this glad tiding is a realization of the divine promise, and therefore has some metaphysical aspect unbound by empirical experience. Still, its fulfillment is conditioned on human exertion. God the Almighty says,

> *Indeed this Quran guides to what is most upright, and gives the good news to the faithful who do righteous deeds that there is a great reward for them.[10]*
>
> *As for those who stay clear of the worship of fake deities and turn penitently to God, there is good news for them. So give good news to My servants who listen to the word [of God] and follow the best [interpretation] of it. They are the ones whom God has guided, and it is they who possess intellect.[11]*
>
> *Announce to the faithful the good news that there will be for them a great grace from God.[12]*

* * *

From this standing principle in Islamic thought, and with the glad tidings provided in the Holy Book and the prophetic traditions of the impending and encompassing relief that will

---

[10] The Holy Quran, 17:9.

[11] The Holy Quran, 39:18.

[12] The Holy Quran, 33:47.

fill the earth with justice after it has been filled with injustice and oppression.... From this principle and these glad tidings, the Commander of the Faithful sees the rays of hope in the future, and he would give glad tidings of an assured and doubtless relief.

The course of history demands it. The promise of God assures it, and God never fails a promise.

The Imam's vision of the course of history was not limited to disaster and catastrophe – as may seem to be the case from a cursory look at *the Peak of Eloquence*. Rather, it is filled with glad tidings as well. We presented some of this in the sections on suffering and reform.

The Imam's vision was precise, specific, bright, and clear-cut.

He saw all this within the larger framework and fundamental movements in the course of history – even if he did not provide details. Amongst those is his vision of a just revolution that cannot be extinguished despite the accumulation of the winds and tides against it.

When God gave the Commander of the Faithful victory over the enemy at the Battle of Jamel, one of his comrades said to him,

> *I wish my brother... had been present and he too would have seen what success and victory God has given you. The Commander of the Faithful asked, 'Did your brother*

hold me as a leader?' When the man replied in the affirmative, Imam Ali said, [In that case he was with us. Rather] in this army of ours individuals are present who are still in the loins of men and wombs of women. Shortly, time will bring them out and faith will get strength through them.[13]

The great coming hope that the Imam gives glad tidings of will be manifested in a universal revolution that corrects the circumstances of the Muslim nation first, and then the circumstances of the entire world. It will be led by a man from the household of the Prophet (s) – he is Imam Mahdi. There are relatively few texts within *the Peak of Eloquence* that specify the character of this grand hope.

This includes his words, "… until God brings out for you one who would collect you together and unite you after disunity."[14]

The belief in the Mahdi is a standing principle that all Muslims agree about. The Quran referred to it in a number of verses. It is the subject of hundreds of recurrent traditions from the Prophet (s) and the Imams from his Household.

Ibn Abi Al-Hadid said in commentary on the foregoing quote,

Then God will bring out for them one who would collect and gather them, referencing a man from the Household.

---

[13] The Peak of Eloquence, Sermon 12.
[14] Al The Peak of Eloquence, Sermon 100.

260

This is a reference to the Mahdi that appears at the end of times. To our [scholars from the Sunni schools of thought], he is not yet in existence and will come to existence later. As for the Imamiyya, he is currently present.[15]

In commentary on another similar text, Ibn Abi Al-Hadid said,

If it were said 'Who is this promised man about whom [Ali] said, "may my father be sacrificed for the son of the best of maids"?' The reply would be, 'As for the Imamiyya, they claim that he is the Twelfth Imam and that he is the son of a maid called Narjis. As for our [scholars from the Sunni schools of thought], they claim that he is a Fatimid and will be born in the future to a maid, and therefore is not present at the time.

Another of the texts from *the Peak of Eloquence* regarding this matter reads,

Beware, it will be tomorrow and the morrow will come soon with things which you do not know. The governor, not from this crowd, will take to task all those were formerly appointed for their ill deeds and the earth will pour forth its eternal treasures and fling before him easily her keys. He will show you the just way of behavior and revive the Quran and traditions, which have become lifeless.[16]

---

[15] Ibn Abi Al-Hadid, *Sharh Nahj Al-Balagha*, 7:94.
[16] The Peak of Eloquence, Sermon 138.

This bright hope is not of an immediate event – if it were to be seen through the view of individual hopes. Death may pass individuals before they delight their eyes with the fulfillment of this hope. To them, as individuals, it is far, far away.

Similarly, it is also distant to any community taken singularly. Centuries may pass and a community may still not be able to achieve in its system and institutions this grand hope.

Yet this hope, if seen relative to the history of mankind as a species, is near. The events that change the course of human history cannot be measured against the lives of individual men, factions, or communities. They cannot be measured in light of the course of history in this or that aspect. Rather, they can be measured only with what befits mankind as a species, in light of the trajectory of universal history.

A thousand years, for example, is a long time if compared to the lifetime of an individual. The same can be said of the course of history in a specific community. But a thousand years is a short time if regarded in the grand scheme of the history of the human race and in comparison to the time needed for major historical shifts – shifts that introduce fundamental changes to the trajectory of the history of the human species and lifts it from one status to another greater in quality. The span required for major historical shifts – as we know – takes thousands of years. Rather, they take tens of thousands of years. This is the grand course of history.[17]

As we wait for the grand course of history to carry humanity to a higher level that it has yet to achieve, this trajectory of history continues – in its smaller movements – to change the circumstances of humans – individuals, groups, societies, and regional factions.

The course of history, in its smaller movements, moves humanity towards the better on a materialistic level. This is proven by empirical reality. But it does not always move humanity towards the better on the moral and spiritual levels. Rather, it may move humanity backwards, as is also proven by empirical reality. This can specifically be seen in the actualities of our modern era.

Responsibility for mankind's regression sits not with fate, but with humanity's will. The world of ethical behavior, whether for the individual or the collective, is not something that is given and ready to be utilized like a prescription drug or mathematical equations. Rather, it is built through the daily

---

[17] Perhaps Ibn Abi Al-Hadid had vaguely imagined such an idea when he said in a commentary to one excerpt of *Nahj Al-Balagha*, "Then he promised them an imminent relief. He said, 'The completion of God's blessings over you, and for you to see what you hope for, is a matter close in time. It is as if it has occurred and become reality.' This is in the same fashion of the divine promises on the Day of Judgment, as divine scriptures all express its proximity, even if we see it to be far. What we precieve as far is close in the knowledge of God. He, the Almighty, said, 'Indeed they see it to be far off, and We see it to be near.' (The Holy Quran, 70:6-7)." Ibn Abi Al-Hadid, *Sharh Nahj Al-Balagha*, 7:95.

struggles of individuals with their regressive whims and desires. It comes through their struggle with their own selves and their attempt to defeat it. The world of ethics is not easily built like the material and empirical world. The world of ethics consists of a constant endeavor for a richer and higher level of humanity. The world of ethics treats the impossible as possible. It is always in a state of regeneration. That is because whenever man reaches a new height of humanity, his eyes will be caught by an even greater and nobler summit to climb.

Therefore, humanity cannot stand still as it waits for the fulfillment of this great hope. Rather, they must act within the smaller movements of history in order to reach new and greater heights than what they have reached through their endeavors.

Thus, Muslims – considering that this great hope will be fulfilled, God willing, by their hand as a faith group, and through their religion of Islam – await this great hope at the forefront of all other faith groups within the greater human community.

Many individuals have attempted to grapple with the issue of the Mahdi and his movement. It is certainly a grand immutable hope promised in the Book of God and our noble traditions, and is assured in the grand trajectory of history. Yet some have concluded that this is a concept of negative impact that hinders development and growth. They claim that it forces stagnation and stops individuals from their movement toward materialistic and moral excellence by promising them salvation through a miracle – a hope that saves man without their participation.

Some of the facts of Muslim history may support this allegation. But the truth is that this twisted negative conception of hope infiltrated the psyche of mankind after a cultural regression that was due to the infiltration of foreign ideas. This regression paralyzed mankind's ability to move forward. It paralyzed mankind's will and effectiveness and changed it into a lethargic and submissive creature.

The truth is much different. To await hope – within this doctrinal context – is an effective and positive form of patience. It is a built on readiness and preparation. It is a constant endeavor that must change the trajectory of Muslim history towards providing the best conditions for the fulfillment and success of this great hope.

We have seen that the course of history – in its smaller movements – does not stop. The quality of this trajectory – ascendant and progressive or descendant and regressive, depending on the quality of ethics and morals – depends on the will of mankind. They are the ones that build their ideal ethical world. It is not built except through positive work motivated by a desire for a better humanity.

* * *

The salutations of God to Muhammad (s) and his Holy Household, and the companions who followed him in righteousness, until the Day of Judgment. And God's salutations to the most celebrated of believers, Ali the Commander of the Faithful (s)

And Praise be to God, Lord of the realms.